Escaping Nothing

Breaking The Clutches Of Anxiety To Have A Life Of Everything

Erica Rose Goldsmith, INHC, CIHC, H.C.

Copyright – Escaping Nothing: Breaking The Clutches Of Anxiety To Have A Life Of Everything by Erica Rose Goldsmith

Copyright © 2017 by Erica Rose Goldsmith

The content of this book is for general instruction only and is based solely on my personal experiences with anxiety. Each person's physical, emotional, and spiritual condition is unique. Any instruction in this book is not intended to replace or interrupt the reader's relationship with a physician, therapist or other professional. Please consult your doctor or therapist for matters pertaining to your specific health, diet, physical and mental needs. Before attempting any physical activity please consult with a physician. This book is not meant to be used to diagnose, treat or cure any mental or physical health condition or illness. There is no guarantee from the author or publisher that the strategies and information provided in this book will help the reader with any condition, symptom or illness. Neither the author nor publisher is responsible for any negative experiences due to the reader following any strategies, information or guidance provided in this book.

All rights reserved. No part of this publication may be reproduced, distributed, or transmitted in any form or by any means, including photocopying, recording, or other electronic or mechanical methods, without the prior written permission of the publisher or author, except in the case of brief quotations embodied in critical reviews and certain other noncommercial uses permitted by copyright law. For permission requests, email the publisher or author at erica@reviveandrenewyou.com

To contact the publisher, visit www.reviveandrenewyou.com

To contact the author, visit www.reviveandrenewyou.com

ISBN-13: 978-0692973455 (Revive & Renew You)
ISBN-10: 0692973451

Library of Congress Control Number: 2017963836
Revive & Renew You, Austin, TX

Photography Back Cover: Jana Perenchio of Brown-Eyed Girl Photography {Schertz, TX}

Printed in the United States of America

Table Of Contents

Dedication	5
Acknowledgements	7
Foreword	9
Introduction	13
Chapter 1: My Story	17
Part I: The Beginning	17
Part II: The Darkness	31
Part III: Reality, Revival, and Recovery	39
Chapter 2: Self-Love	43
Chapter 3: Self-Care	47
Chapter 4: Gratitude Journal	51
Chapter 5: Morning Pages Journal	55
Chapter 6: Meditation	61
Chapter 7: Essential Oils	65
Chapter 8: Acupressure	69
Chapter 9: Acupuncture	73

Chapter 10: Mindfulness — 77

Chapter 11: Yoga — 83

Chapter 12: Re-Framing — 87

Chapter 13: Medication — 93

Chapter 14: Coloring, Drawing, and Painting — 102

Chapter 15: Dancing — 107

Chapter 16: Morning Wake-Up Song — 111

Chapter 17: Stretching — 115

Chapter 18: Exercise — 119

Chapter 19: Vision Boards — 123

Chapter 20: Therapists (all of them) — 127

Chapter 21: Post-It Notes — 131

Chapter 22: Where I Am Now — 135

Chapter 23: Keeping Up With The Routine, What Happens If You Stop? — 139

Conclusion — 141

About The Author — 143

Dedication

This book is dedicated to the younger version of myself and anyone in the world out there who is like her. May this book bring you comfort in knowing you are not alone. May this book bring tears of relief in knowing that what you feel is real and you can have a chance at life. May this book be your voice that might have gone unheard until now.

I wish you strength, power and the most ultimate sense of endurance. You have it. I am sure of it, because you have already survived this long.

Acknowledgements

Thank you to all my family and friends who have stood by me even when I pushed away. Thank you to anyone who has ever shared their story with me so I didn't feel alone. Hopefully this book can help you in return to find other ways to continue on your journey of fighting anxiety. You all are my everything and I can only hope to be as good of a person to you as you all have been to me. Thank you to any naysayers for pushing me to the point where I couldn't keep quiet anymore.

A special thanks to my family who were in the trenches with me like no other. Who understood and accepted that it was necessary for me to heal alone in order to heal fully. We are a force. Mom, there needs to be a new word invented for the level of thanks you deserve. You have proved to be one of the strongest people I know. James, you're my whole heart. I will always be your biggest fan and protector. Josh, we couldn't be more different, yet we share a bond of camaraderie in silence the way only siblings can. Thanks for sticking up for me when I needed it. Dad, I'm happy you have found your happy. It looks good on you, keep up the hard work. Nana, my guardian angel with an endless bowl of candy, thank you for your love and Pop-Pop, I'll always take with me the lesson of the mirror. You've shown me to never lose sight of myself and much more. I've loved you all, through it all. Thanks for waiting by my side, whether it was in silence or anger while I figured this life out.

Sandi, Thank you for everything you've done. Time for us to celebrate! Kay, Chapter 10 is for you. I'm forever grateful for you and your distinct methods and approach. Gina, Thank you for all of your guidance through school and all of our projects.

Thanks for leading me to believe that any — let alone all — of this was even possible. Pamela, Thank you for your confidence, motivation, and accountability. Finally, Thanks to everyone who reached out to tell me a little bit about yourself and your experience with anxiety. You all kept me going by helping me realize how important this book could be, how necessary it is to start the conversation, and just how many of us there are out there. I value your braveness to share your story with me with such ease. I hope this book helps all of you to find some more resolve if needed. Love.

Foreword

You cannot always control what goes on outside.
But you can always control what goes on inside.
Dr. Wayne Dyer

Mental health challenges clearly still have a huge stigma, probably because they are not understood and at times very difficult to manage. Fixing them is often not even the goal, managing them may be the way to go. However, individuals who struggle with depression, anxiety, or trauma very often feel defeated due to their seemingly everlasting difficulties and the lack of knowledge of how to deal with their symptoms. The judgment they feel coming from family, friends, and strangers can even discourage them from openly looking for outside help.

Psychotherapy can have many different faces. For me it has always been a place where clients not only share their experiences and feelings in order to be able to put them into perspective, but also find an abundance of coping skills that help them to literally change their lives. These coping skills include ways of physical self-care, including nutrition and exercise, dealing with emotional stress and relationships in their lives, changing their thought processes to stop fighting themselves, others, and the world every day, and spiritual development. We need to find balance in our lives and actively pursue our own happiness to eventually achieve it.

Clients need to determine which of the suggestions made in therapy truly work for them. They need to try them out and give them a chance by applying them consistently over a certain period of time. Every client is different and may respond in their own way. Therapists are not all-knowing, they only guide their clients towards a path of self-help and empowerment. It is the clients who have to do the work, and that can feel overwhelming at times. It is their responsibility to help themselves by picking and choosing tools out of the toolbox they are putting together in a joint effort during the therapy process. Therapists can neither fix clients nor make sure that clients in fact apply the skills developed together.

I personally have seen clients who came into my office, learned the skills they needed, and literally ran with them. They took responsibility, empowered themselves, and worked so hard that I may have had to see them four to six times only to get them back in charge of their thoughts, feelings, and life in general. Then there are other clients who want to be fixed, who want the therapist to do the work, and it may take a little while to get them to work with me until they finally take control of their healing process. Another group of clients tends to state that nothing is working, but when I check in with them they eventually admit that they have not applied the skills they agreed to practice since their previous session consistently or at all. There may be denial and learned helplessness that needs to be resolved first before clients are able to truly do their work in therapy, which consists of constant effort to make certain skills part of a daily routine such as eating, drinking, and sleeping.

Erica Goldsmith's book on how to combat anxiety and panic attacks is a heartfelt account of her own lifelong experiences and struggles with these mental disorders, and how she managed to move towards a life of empowerment and happiness. In her own warm personal voice, she tries to encourage others to go from feeling defeated to building up their own strength and determination, so they can gain control and find joy in their lives they may have never had before. In a clear and practical manner, she talks the reader through a series of coping skills that have worked for her. Her compilation of tools that have helped her to overcome the depths of her anxiety and panic disorder when she started applying them consistently as part of her daily routine is a beautiful confirmation that therapy works when clients are provided the knowledge and skills to help themselves. Unfortunately, Erica herself, as she points out in her story, did not find this kind of help in therapy for a long time and sadly had to figure things out mostly on her own until she finally found a professional who introduced an approach that worked for her. This fact alone needs to be a wake-up call for all therapists to make their work as personalized and practical as possible so that their clients can benefit most from this joint venture. After all, our dedication to help others is why we are in this profession in the first place.

Alexandra M. Asirvadam, MA, LPC, LCDC, INHC
Licensed Professional Counselor
Licensed Chemical Dependency Counselor
Integrative Nutrition Health Coach
Author of Balanced Bodies: A holistic approach to happiness

Waxahachie, TX
www.amacounseling.com

Introduction

For as long as I can remember I've always enjoyed making others happy. If I saw someone upset, bothered, hurt, or just not in a good mood, I considered it my job to help them feel better. I've always been told I was a good listener and a giver of sage advice. The more I was told I was good at making people feel happy, the more I pursued it, even to my own detriment. I was a "yes" person even when it didn't benefit me and I was a people pleaser even if it meant dragging myself through the mud with no air left in my lungs. To put my own oxygen mask on before helping others was a foreign thing to me and one I most definitely didn't practice. When I couldn't help others, it would crush me. I would feel like a failure and that I had let them down. On a regular basis this would leave me feeling defeated, unimportant, and only reassured that I wasn't "needed". It wouldn't be until my 30's that I would finally learn where this need to please stemmed from. I had had severe anxiety and panic disorder since the age of four, and these behaviors were a result of my mental illness and me trying to hide it, and that nearly killed me.

The first thirty-some years of my life I would spend suffering from severe anxiety, panic attacks, bouts of hibernation away from people and life, entertaining constant irrational thoughts, ideas and even negative self-talk. I would try what I thought was "everything out there" including medications and different therapists along the way but none would help or even really put a dent in my misery. I would be surrounded by people who claimed to have anxiety and who would say, "just deal with it," or "just calm down, stop worrying," or "I have anxiety too, you just have to learn to relax," and I would believe them. I would think, "I don't need help, this is just something people deal with and I too will figure it out one day, I guess." Well, I was wrong, and so were they. What I would come to realize is yes, many people have anxiety; however, not all anxiety is created equal and not every person reacts the same way to it. That's what has brought me here.

Throughout this book you will learn first of my personal experience with anxiety disorder — how long I've had it, symptoms I've had, how bad it really got, and things I've experienced first hand along with what I've learned about this illness. I've included plenty of metaphors to help us really understand what's going on in our minds as well. For those who maybe don't have it as severe, or necessarily at all, I try my best to help you understand how deep this mental illness can go and to help you maybe have some compassion for someone you know who suffers from anxiety or to help you know and feel what it can be like.

Then comes the good part. I cover 20 different techniques and tools I use to help combat anxiety and that help me continue to maintain a level of control over my anxiety that I never knew existed. With each example I first explain in my own words what it is, and my thoughts on it. Then, I explain why I think it works or what it did for me and why that helped with my anxiety. I also include variations of these techniques as well as how to incorporate them into your daily routine. The only thing I have really left out is the science. I have left this angle out because there are so many sources that I didn't want to lean one way and not the other. Some definitions and science are mixed with opinions and I wanted this to be solely my perspective, so the definitions of these techniques that I list are not technical. They are my take on it via what I've learned, and gathered through my own experience without anything added. During these chapters you'll find some redundancy as far as "what it is," or "how it helps you," and "how to incorporate it," and that's for two reasons. One, a lot of these techniques do the same thing, they just go about different ways of accomplishing it and I have found that instead of doing repetitions of one technique, I found better results by doing a little of each technique while using multiple techniques at once. The benefits and how they work might be similar and seem repetitive but trust that each method deserves its own spotlight and has its own power. Second, if you're at all like me, you learn best by repetition so if each chapter says the same sentence, know that it's intentional. It's to make sure you really get the point and to drive home how important that step is.

I show you how I discovered happiness and that the ability to sleep for 8 hours is a real thing, as is the ability to focus and move past trauma. I explain each one all while helping you to hopefully build your own daily routine to help you get to a place where life is a little easier. The goal is for you to use this book to hand pick a few techniques to start and slowly build up to where you're doing almost all of them every single day. I ask that when you commit to a technique, that you at least commit to it for a month. After that, you can give it fair judgement on whether or not it worked for you and then choose to keep it in your routine or to dismiss it.

Another purpose of this book is to really show support to everyone. From those who have zero anxiety or nervousness at all to those who only experience a glimmer of what I do, all the way to those who have full blown panic attacks where their hands and joints lock up, hyperventilating ensues, they vomit uncontrollably and with the worst of them, they lose control of their bowels. Sound horrible? Well, that's because it is. Too graphic? Well, get used to it. This is the brutal truth of severe anxiety and panic disorder.

Chapter 1

My Story

Part I

The Beginning

If you could have any superpower, what would it be? This is a common ice breaker or conversation starter that many reply with far-fetched, non-realities like "The ability to fly," "To be invisible," or even "Time-traveling." I used to want to be a mind reader which, as I grew older, I learned the drive behind was almost solely so that I could view other people's opinions of me. How insecure of me, at even such a young age to turn something magical into something that was once again, decision-based off my anxiety. Some could think being this self-aware would have me answering to a different tune, but it doesn't. Instead, it has me wishing for a bigger "power". If I could have any superpower in the world, it would be to make all "invisible" disease and illness, visible. This goes from the person like myself with severe anxiety and panic disorder to the people with chronic migraines and fibromyalgia to the autoimmune diseases, MS and PTSD. All of them, visible. As visible as a broken bone sticking out of a person's leg or a 3rd degree burn. Brutally and gut-wrenchingly visible.

Someone's having a panic attack, you see it. A friend is suicidal, you see it. A co-worker needs a mental health day, you see it. Your relative has PTSD, you see it. Your teenager is depressed, you see it. You see all of it.

A while ago I suffered over nine fractures in both of my shoulder blades and in two vertebrae in my neck, amidst many other injuries that come along with breaking bones. The muscle damage, tendons, ligaments, bruising and bumps, I had it all. It was a nightmare. You might have even cringed at just the thought when reading that sentence. But what about when you read the sentence about me having severe anxiety disorder or that I suffered from panic attacks? Unless you've been there, there's not much cringing going on and this is what I've always had a hard time accepting. This is the drive of this book. To help everyone, with or without anxiety to develop a deeper understanding of what this mental illness can be like.

During the years of healing from my injuries so many people would ask, "What happened?" I would explain and every single person would react the same. They'd shrug up their shoulders and cringe and even make a face similar to them having just bit into a lemon or having witnessed something horrible. Some would even bring their hands to their heart and gasp. Some would cup their mouths and say, "Oh my gosh!" Some have even said my story made them emotional and followed with a, "Thank you for being an inspiration," which is when the question would hit me. I wondered what percentage of people I was talking to had experienced a broken bone before, thus justifying their reactions to my story and truly knowing my pain. I bet it's not 100% of them. So for the ones who hadn't shared this experience, how is it that these people are able to so easily empathize with me and almost feel my pain, within a few seconds of me telling the story? The only answer that entered my mind is that they've seen pictures of broken bones or they've suffered other types of injuries so they can imagine a scale of how a worse injury could feel worse and therefore sympathize accordingly. They've seen the athlete on the field with a bone protruding the skin, the blood and x-rays. Also, there are just things one can experience that are known to be extremely painful. Giving birth, suffering burns, a bullet wound, passing a kidney stone, and breaking a bone are some examples known to all be very painful things to experience physically.

So there you have it, a physical pain scale and therefore an ability to feel someone else's pain even if you've never been there yourself. We have the ability to imagine it. The question then begs to ask, why don't we have a mental pain scale for illnesses that people are equally sympathetic to? Again, the only thought that entered my mind is the visual aspect of it. You can't see it. Perhaps out-of-sight out-of-mind is at play here. Perhaps it's the lack of discussion due to people being embarrassed that they have a mental illness. Maybe the lack of discussion is the people who are scared that by bringing it to light, it somehow will give it magical powers and make it worse or give everyone anxiety. This is simply ridiculous. Perhaps over time people have abused the ability to use these mental illnesses as an excuse for something or have cried wolf one too many times and thus now it is sometimes viewed less intense and taken far less serious than it ought to be. I mean, how dare we give attention to those in need mentally, right? Attention and medical services to the crazies out there, and run the risk of feeding this beast and making it worse. Well, I can assure you that's not how my anxiety works. In fact it's the complete opposite and I have yet to personally meet someone who feels differently. Maybe it's a combination of it all. Either way, I'm not a fan and I'm tired of the broom hitting me, trying to push me back under the rug. Here's a look into where it all started and perhaps I can give you an idea of just what it can be like.

I have lived with severe anxiety disorder and panic attacks my whole life. The earliest and most vivid memory I can recall happened in kindergarten. I was called from the classroom and led down the hallway. I had no idea what I did or why I was in "trouble," but the staff member of the school kept saying, "where have you been, they're all waiting for you. They're running late now because of you." I had no clue what she was talking about but I could feel myself getting hotter and my heart starting to race. I didn't know what was happening or where she was taking me. I, for some reason, felt so guilty — to a level a 5 year-old shouldn't even know possible. She opened the door to the room and announced, "Here she is, I'm not sure what happened but you can start now."

The teacher motioned to a desk and told me in front of everyone, "I'll get to you but for now please just sit down and be quiet while I get everyone else started." I still had no clue what was going on and all I could think of was how much trouble I was in or whether or not I was going to get in even more trouble when I got home later. What was I doing here? Why were the lights dimmed? Why is everyone older and bigger than me? Everyone's looking at me. Am I in trouble? Before I knew it these spinning thoughts became more than just thoughts, they became physical. The anxiety flipped to panic and I lost control. In just five seconds I had thrown up all over my desk and soiled my pants. Yup. I then raised my hand and with tears in my eyes I said, "I, um, I got sick." The teacher and all the kids gasped and started holding their noses which brought about an entirely new level of anxiety and embarrassment. I was removed from the room and taken to the front office where I would sit in my "mess" until my mom arrived. No one cleaned me up, no one said anything. I just sat there while the lady at the desk fanned herself to keep the odor at a distance. My mom arrived shortly and to my surprise didn't yell at me at all. Instead she yelled at the secretary for just letting me "sit there like that." She said, "Why did no one at least change her clothes with lost and found items? Something?!?" I swear I gave a dirty look with my puke-covered face to the secretary as we walked out. Years later, I would find out that what happened was that my teacher in kindergarten had noticed I was progressing fast and they wanted to have me tested for advanced classes. The classroom I was taken to was full of fifth graders — I was meant to take the same test as them to see how I scored. My kindergarten teacher was supposed to send me to the classroom at the designated time but I was the only kindergartner going, so it had slipped her mind. That's all it was, a silly test, but because I was in the dark about what was happening in the moment, I panicked.

These attacks feel like mini traumas (which technically I guess they are). The body and mind suffer and go through a recovery period afterwards. Panic attacks can wear you out and leave you drained while mentally, you're still not even sure what has happened in the first place.

This would be the first of many, many instances throughout my life that would unfortunately end like this. Yup, not the best memory or the most fun thing to experience in a day of a kindergartener. That's just it though, this illness didn't care that I was a fragile five year-old, it was taking its course no matter what. That day in the classroom was embarrassing beyond belief. It's one thing to be nervous about something, but this was a whole new ball game with the nerves and thoughts. I had zero control over my mind or body and at that age, had no clue what was going on or even how to explain it to someone.

We all have anxiety on some level or another. Like all emotions, all humans experience them, the only difference is to what extent. Some worry about an exam or job interview and shake it off and that's the worst it gets for them. Others have anxiety about their doctor's visits to the point of avoidance or they experience some physical symptoms like fainting at the smallest sign or even mention of blood. Some have anxiety only as a child, then it fades as they get older and learn more about how the world works. For others it is the polar opposite and anxiety is something that enters their life as they get older and learn more about the world. For me, it started bad, then it got really ugly and then it got nearly lethal. I hovered at nearly lethal for about as long as a human body could and to this day, I'm not completely sure why. Perhaps it was a necessary step for me, to hold on to that person for as long as I could to make sure that the old part of me couldn't co-exist with my new lifestyle. Knowing that once I combatted it, it had to be for good was a scary thought. That old part of me was still me, it was all I knew, so in a sense I can understand why it was so hard for me to let her go. I was so afraid that letting her go would let go of other parts of me that I loved. How would my mind know how to keep the good parts and only let the bad ones go? This back and forth went on for about five years before I was able to realize that quite frankly, any part of the old me that would leave via being attached to the anxiety, I wouldn't want and for just that reason. It was still attached to my anxiety. It would be toxic and consistently try to drag me backwards. This revelation of the fact that it was ok to let go of her was my everything and it's why I share my story. I want to help as many as I can who might be in, or might be approaching, the nearly lethal phase and who need any and all help they can get to break out of it before it gets too late. I am not suggesting that this book take the place of any other methods used but more as an additive to what you are already doing to help yourself.

As far as I've been informed no one has ever died from a panic attack. My argument there, is that there is probably no mention of things people have done to deal with anxiety and what those "thing's" side effects could do to someone. That's where it's terrifying to me. In these attacks you become at the mercy of your body. You can't control your thoughts and your body goes into a fight-or-flight response as if you're being attacked by a bear. You are convinced you are dying. No one can tell you otherwise, and in that moment you are willing to do just about anything to get it to stop. I mean anything. The sensation and belief that you're dying is so vivid and convincing that you'll do anything to get it to stop because in your mind, you're going to die anyway. You can experience hundreds of panic attacks but somehow when it's present you're sure that that's the one that's going to finally kill you.

For those who have never experienced a panic attack, I'll try to paint a picture that is the best I've been able to come up with in my journeys of talking to others. I believe most, if not all, of us at one time have slept through our alarms whether for school or work. You go from a sound sleep to waking up, looking at the clock and realizing you're already supposed to be somewhere, to the stomach-dropping, hot flash, heart-racing, can't move fast enough freak-out mode all in a matter of 3 seconds before leaping out of bed. Imagine that very feeling only add that when you try to get out of bed, you realize you're actually in a coffin, buried 6 feet underground somehow still alive, yet you're running out of air as you start to hear a creak and feel some dirt crumble onto your face. Imagine how that would feel and multiply it by 100 and picture how stuck and helpless you would feel. How fast before you give up? I mean you fully believe you're going to die it's just a matter of how long it's going to take. Now imagine inside that coffin are some options. Continue to freak out until you run out of air or the coffin collapses in on you, drink some numbing medicine so you could at least die comfortably, or just die. This is panic. This is what an attack is like, and they are not short either. Do you see now how when someone says, "just relax," it can make your head want to explode?

Now imagine this feeling exactly the same only all you're doing is trying to make it through the TSA line so you can get on the airplane to go on vacation. Awful right? Well, that's often the worst part about them is that you can be in your happy place, lying on the beach on vacation not a care in the world — or so you think — and for some reason your mind and body will decide to have a panic attack. Usually they are triggered, the TSA can be an easy example, however the trigger can happen plenty of time — sometimes days — before the attack actually happens making it borderline impossible to nail all of your triggers down. This is why this illness is so evil. It can come out when you least expect it. When you aren't looking, "it" is. It is always looking, and that's part of why it's so hard to beat. It's always one step ahead because it knows all your next moves.

You would know if you've had a panic attack before, but anxiety can be a little hard to diagnose and usually you'll want a professional involved to do so and to inform you of what to do next. If you think you have it and it's affecting your life, you can start with your primary care physician or even go straight to a psychologist or psychiatrist, someone who can properly diagnose you as well as confirm the severity of it. This will help you to begin your path by knowing what you're up against as well as help give you a starting point for your healing journey.

Once you know you have it, you don't have to scream it from the roof tops — although you'll find in a little bit why I recommend doing that — you don't even have to initially talk about it with anyone besides a professional. Anxiety is an awful, awful feeling. It's not a thing we can see or touch. It is simply a feeling, a way of being, and that is what can make it so unbearable. It isn't for the faint of heart so having someone walking you through it is crucial.

If you have anxiety, odds are that at some point you've been questioned, made to feel like a liar or exaggerator or been forced into playing the medication trial/error game one too many times. You've been told by others that, "it's not real," "you just need to relax," or my personal favorite "I worry too and you don't see me flipping out." Well, let me just say, I get it. I truly understand what it's like having anxiety, so you won't be hearing any of that nonsense here. From losing relationships over it, to losing jobs because of it, and from throwing up in a public trash can to having full on hallucinations, I have experienced a lot.

First things first, you have to accept it. I know this sounds trivial and even obvious but as it will be with most things I cover in this book, we're going to look deeper here. When I say you have to accept it, I mean really accept it, own it and eventually as mentioned, shout it from the mountain tops and practically wear a T-shirt that says, "I have anxiety disorder." Sound horrible? Well, then you're probably an example of someone who has yet to truly accept their fate. Let's expose it for what it is. Every time you reveal its ugly face you are taking away its power. **Anxiety thrives on keeping us isolated and private. Reverse this and it loses some of its power. Take what it is that you're afraid of and let's turn it off.**

Are you afraid people will talk? Let them. They're talking anyway, and they always will, so you might as well be fighting your anxiety while they're off rambling nonsense. You win. Are you afraid that exposing it will make it worse? It won't. It's already so bad that this is one where you need to trust and recognize where you stand right now and the fact that it can't really get any worse, so why not try? For me, exposing it and pulling off the mask gave me so much power! Letting everyone see the devil behind the curtain and exposing him to light made him almost melt away. Again, you win. Are you afraid people won't believe you? Who cares? Let it go! Honestly, listen to this statement, "What if they don't believe me?" That's like telling someone you had a horrible nightmare or are going through a divorce or that you really don't feel well today and they just shrug their shoulders, say, "I highly doubt it's really that bad" or "big deal" and walk away leaving you to crumble. Do you really want that in your life? I hope not. Maybe they don't know how to help you, and that's fine but if they flat out say you're exaggerating, lying or making it up, it's time to set some boundaries and possibly find new members for your circle. There are people out there who understand exactly where you are coming from and exactly what you're going through. What if simply talking about it and exposing it put you in front of these people and therefore you began to start new relationships of love and support? You win. Do you see a theme here? **You win when you begin to acknowledge what's going on in your mind and body and more importantly, you start**

taking care of it. The first step in doing this is acceptance. Full-on, raw, and bold-faced acceptance.

After you have become comfortable in saying it aloud, now it's time to hunker down and find out what makes you happy. It's time to take care of you. This is where the self-care and self-love come into play. By self-care and self-love, I literally mean taking care of yourself and loving yourself. We'll cover these in the next two chapters, but here's an example of how these, amidst the other 18 techniques in this book could possibly help you.

You've probably heard of hundreds of things to do to combat anxiety, right? There's articles, books and remedies by the thousands and if you're like me you've probably tried what feels like them all! Well, I have good news and bad news. Bad news is that with severe cases of anxiety, most of these remedies are like putting a drop of water on a bonfire. They are pointless efforts that dissipate before they even touch the flames. The good news is you can stop worrying that you're a mutant and that for some reason none of these work for you and instead, start understanding why. For each simple activity, it's not that you're doing it wrong or that you didn't do it for months on end. It's that it alone simply isn't enough. Let's break this down.

If you take a friend's advice who says yoga worked for their anxiety and you try it and it doesn't work do you stop to think maybe there's a reason why? No, you have anxiety, of course you wouldn't try to resolve it. Your mind doesn't work that way. You assume it's you and use this as an example of how you're broken or how you are the problem. It takes time but slowly you will realize that this is not true. Here's a few real reasons it doesn't work. It could just be yoga doesn't work for you mentally. Simple as that. There are dozens of exercises out there and for good reason, we're all different so we all need different remedies. It could also be that your body just doesn't flow with it and it's a physical conflict. Again, everyone is different and everyone's body responds differently to everything we do to it. What alleviates one persons anxiety could fuel another's. If someone has mild anxiety, yes, yoga could work wonders. However, for someone else, it's simply not enough. For some people, yoga alone doesn't stand a chance against the demon that is their severe anxiety. So, normally one would try to find something stronger but rarely are successful. How hard are we actually looking though?

Let's stop thinking vertically and start thinking horizontally. Yoga alone isn't enough. So we must build an army. Yoga is powerful, but think of how powerful it could be combined with meditation. Now, think of those two teamed up and toss in another "fighter", journaling. Now you have many drops of water falling onto the bonfire. They're still not enough to put it out, but it's starting to flicker a little. It's getting irritated. So, you guessed it, we add more fighters. Toss in some epsom salt baths, acupuncture and reducing your sugar and caffeine intake and now your army is even larger. Catching on? It kind of makes you feel stronger just thinking about it, no?

Here's where step one comes back in, the acceptance. Here's where you really need to be good at this because we're not here to cure your anxiety. Most likely it will never fully go away. You might never be free of it, and that eventually will also be easier for you to accept and understand. It will always exist on some level, you just have to begin to transform your use of energy to not feed it. You can learn how to take the energy you're using to harbor and hide your anxiety and use it instead on accepting your life and caring for yourself. The fire will never go out. Even if you have a fantastic day, nothing goes wrong, you're smiles all day and you fall sound asleep at night, trust the demons that are your anxiety will be working overtime through the night to get that fire going back so it's ripe and flourishing first thing in the morning for you. However, with a healthy self-care and self-love routine filled with enough techniques all packed in daily, I can almost promise you that one day you will wake up and realize you've had access to a firehose all along ready to tackle each day.

The next several chapters will each explain an activity, tool or technique that I personally have tested out for no less than a month straight, before giving it a yes as to the effect it had and how much it helped my anxiety. You'll read on about these helpful tools and techniques and hopefully begin to not feel alone in this for a minute. Your aim is to come away with a method or two to start trying to help you beat this awful devil of an illness. But before doing that, let's go one level deeper to really unveil what I meant by the bad, the ugly, and the lethal.

Part II

The Darkness

If you have never experienced anxiety here is an uncomfortable and raw look inside. For those who have, here is where I want you to find comfort in knowing you're not alone. Here is where I want you to see that I do understand and that if these tools can help even me, then there truly can be hope for you. There will be lots of metaphors that are personal to me and are not meant to offend or wrongly and unfairly compare any two situations — this is strictly how anxiety makes me feel. Everyone is different and some will completely disagree with some metaphors used to describe the feeling and others will melt into relief, forever moving forward now knowing they're not crazy.

When someone dies, many people say the hardest part of the day is to wake up because for two seconds you're relieved thinking it was a dream and you feel good. Then you remember they're gone, that it was real and instantly the pain sets in. Well, that can be how anxiety feels. Everyday you wake up thinking you're in the wrong life. This can't be real, no one can feel like this. How is everyone else doing it? How does anyone else feel THIS, live THIS, and survive THIS? How am I supposed to keep going? Sometimes I wish anxiety would die. I wake every morning having to remember it wasn't a dream. It's real, it's controlling and I've already lost before the day has even started. That good feeling you feel when your brain is off while you're asleep you don't even get to enjoy because, well, you're asleep. Anxiety has many faces. I like to call them the many faces of the devil. This is not to be confused with psychosis but rather is just meant to help others see the many sides and symptoms anxiety can instill besides just "nervousness". They don't have voices, there is no change in me as a person — like say if you had personality disorder — there is just an extreme emotion that steps forward at any given moment and sometimes for absolutely no reason. I'll share just a few of what I personally deal with and have had to learn to control and try to stop before they get to the foreground.

Frustration:

Anxiety could be compared to being a toddler who's trying to express something but doesn't know how yet or who has yet to learn to speak. For an adult this can be like being in a foreign country where you don't speak the language. It's like being color blind where no matter how many times someone tells you something is green, all you see is red. After time, you learn to understand that it is green, but no matter how hard you try, all you will ever see is red. This can be frustrating beyond belief. You don't understand why others don't see things the way you do or believe that you truly can't understand them. Arguments become invalid and pointless. Explaining things can be tough and even understanding things can be intimidating because all the information is coming in differently. To say this is a cause for feeling like you're different from the get-go is an understatement.

Parents of children with anxiety possibly will notice their children lashing out, expressing abnormal behavior — usually bad behavior coming from a normally well-mannered child — or even the child beginning to tell lies. All of this possibly is for one reason. Attention. Until they reach a certain age, it is basically impossible for a child to understand what anxiety is. Even when they get to an age to understand it, that doesn't mean they can handle it or know what to do about it. Therefore the reactions they exhibit can truly be uncontrolled and unintentional. In that moment all they know is that negative behaviors can inevitably get more attention than positive actions. So, in an episode of anxiousness or panic they will lash out and do whatever they need to do to get attention to find resolve. This initial cause of the actions however, is never expressed. The reason for the behavior is rarely explained and talked about and therefore remains unresolved. It goes dismissed as bad behavior or a child just "being a child". If your child seems in need often, try to find out why. Yes, it absolutely could just be them being a child, however on the off chance that it's more than that, you'll be glad you looked a little bit deeper. A good reference here is if the behavior lasts for more than two weeks. A child can have on and off moments of course; however, if their behavior is consistently off for a period longer than two weeks it might be a good time to tune it and pay a little closer attention. Your advocacy will be all they have in the beginning.

Hopelessness:

After enough frustration, then comes the loss of all hope. You've stopped believing in all the protective emotions like love, trust, and sympathy. When you don't believe these really exist, then you've also stopped believing there's anything to protect you. You're wide open for attack. Vulnerable to the max. No shield in a world of sharp objects. Getting hurt is inevitable, getting destroyed is a given. When you feel so strongly you're going to get hurt no matter what, you begin thinking, "Why bother?"

Perfectionism:

Perfection is our only acceptance. Anything less is not for us and we have failed and thus fall. Because perfection doesn't exist, guess how often we are falling. It's non stop. It's worse than getting kicked while you're down. We start to build our life around this disease instead of building our life with it. Or better yet, building our life in spite of it. We stay away from the spontaneous things. We play it safe. We don't dare to be free and have fun because what if we get it wrong. We're already hurting so why risk hurting more. Why? Then when we do push beyond it and it doesn't work or we fail we only go deeper. We only see that we were right and have some sick sense of proof that we weren't crazy. That it did happen — the bad stuff. So why not keep thinking about the bad stuff to prevent it from happening in the first place. So we make sure to not attempt anything we can't be "perfect" at.

Self-sabotage:

Self-sabotage is our MO. Anytime someone does even the smallest favor we feel indebted for life. It's an endless feeling of repayment and giving back because we didn't deserve their kindness. We don't know how to accept things therefore we truly never do. This then deprives us of so much joy than if we had just accepted these small gifts to begin with. We don't ask for help. When help is forced upon us we feel weak. We feel the person resents having to help us and we try to eliminate any circumstance where that could even happen to begin with. We make life so difficult for ourselves but again, chaos is a comfort zone for us and so we sabotage our lives so that this is the norm at all times. On the outside it may seem that we're ok, we're free and just like others. But we're not. We're prisoners of our own minds and so are our bodies. No one has the key to this mental prison except us, yet we can't get out and there is no off switch. 24/7 solitary confinement inside our own minds of negative, paranoid, exaggerating thoughts. Awful right? It is, yet we do it to ourselves over and over. Sometimes we'll even create the chaos out of nothing so we can feel at home and comfortable for just a little bit.

Isolation:

We try to never allow anyone to see our true weakness and vulnerability, or at least that's what we think. It's extreme and violent and no one wants that tainted image. The image of the devil. We have to hide it, put on a smile, and pull ourselves up by the bootstraps. Any idea how exhausting it is to hide the devil 24/7 and put on that fake smile? Any idea how frustrating it is then when you are this exhausted yet you still can't sleep at night. It's a full time job. It never goes away, there is no off switch. You get moments of peace, but that's followed by a quick tap on the shoulder to remind you he's still there immediately after. You think the only way to kill the devil inside is to kill yourself. To cut yourself open and let him bleed out of you. Or to succumb to it, just surrender and see how far it goes. How deep could you possibly get engulfed? Let's just say that neither of these is the answer. Neither is even close.

Comfort Zone:

Like I've said, tragedy is our home. We love it. It sounds awful but chaos is familiar and it's what we grew up feeling. So chaos and tragedy feel like home. We cry at the most unimportant things and then the actual tragedies we are almost numb to. We expect these tragedies all the time, so when they actually happen, it's like they surprise us less. It's what we've been worrying about and when it arrives there's a brief comfort that we were right. We saw it coming. The numbness tragedy causes us lets us be quiet for a moment in the sense that we finally feel connection. It's comfortable for us, it's where we live in our heads. I wasn't always crying at a funeral, yet at other times would latch onto a story or situation so I could use it as an excuse to feel something later on. For us to feel things for no reason was negative, weak, and frowned upon. So we'll highlight these events or even hold onto them for a later date so when we have an episode we then feel our actions are ok and more importantly, justified. For us, life has been a disappointment of tragedies and deaths of emotions, hopes, and dreams. Anything relative even in an irrational sense, is familiar and therefore something we relish in. It's sick, embarrassing, and horrible. But for some, it is our real mind. This backwards manner of emotional processing and releasing is something that only adds to the problems we have. No matter how embarrassing these behaviors are, we have to remember the importance of accepting them.

Paranoia:

Paranoia? Yeah, that one's in there too. It'll have you going to the darkest of places where you forget who you are. You'll even question being a human, like you're in a movie. You're thinking it's all a set up and you're the bait. They're all watching, laughing, and following the script. You're the TV show that is their entertainment. That's why they don't believe you. They have to keep the play going, they have to keep reading their lines. They have to keep you believing. Believing that there's nothing wrong with you. That's what they're paid to do. They're watching you through the other side of the mirrors.

They listen to you through the air vents. They all talk about you behind your back and are only nice to you because then they have a role in the play. This voice gets louder and louder the more you listen. Telling you the devil is inside, he equals red and red equals blood. So blood must be shed to release him. Not on others but on yourself. But you're not suicidal. So you begin to want to be. You sickly envy someone who has done the deed in knowing they listened and you understand why. You'll never do it, because you genuinely don't want to die. You'll never do it, but when you hear someone committed suicide, you'll also always understand why. Paranoia can be a major driving force here and the thoughts as you can see get out of control before you can even blink. In this manner, yes, we do have irrational thoughts and most of us are completely aware of this, which is why when people accuse us of being irrational at other times it can be extremely insulting and hurtful.

Sadness:

You never want to die you just want it to stop. You want to be able to be awake and not have your brain going. You can become obsessed with sleep because it's a shut off. To help you sleep, alcohol or drugs can be dangerous, even deadly — as can any downer. You just want it to stop and although you'd never kill yourself, you also begin to question if you would care if you died. How do you explain that to someone? The answer is we don't. We keep it inside and try to figure it out because that's what we were told to do. We were told to stop being silly. That, "It isn't that bad, grow up," or to "stop being such a baby," a whiner, complainer or irrational exaggerator. So then we just stop. We isolate all the time, turtles in our shells and mentally going into the corner when we need to. We stop talking, being, and showing up because we feel no one is really there with us anyway. When they say they are, you question them. As bad as they can possibly imagine it is, you question if they really get it. Because if they did, they'd never question you. In this back and forth we find ourselves facing sadness. We're not lonely, but we do feel alone in our world.

Part III

Reality, Revival, and Recovery

Trying to hurt ourselves is never intentional — like I've said, we don't want to die. But we do have moments of not caring if we do die to the point where it is the scariest hell you can ever encounter. Then one day we realize we cannot fight death. When we're supposed to go, we will go no matter the situation. When we're not meant to go, we will continue to survive these moments of hell over and over again and end up being the story others repeat as the miracles that happen. We begin to stop obsessing over it, to stop worrying about it, and to stop trying to control it. This life or death thing, it's not our call. This becomes a reality check eventually for us and we are awakened with a means to find a way to just be.

"I will never leave you in the weaknesses of your illness," "It will never scare me enough to leave." Even if people have said these things to me, I myself needed them to leave. I needed to face life alone and head-on. I needed to know that I could completely fall to the bottom of the barrel and have only one breath left and still come back — all while being alone. I had to prove to myself I didn't need anyone so that in case they did run, in case my illness was too scary for them, I would already be prepared for it and know I'd be just fine. Why I went this route I will never understand and I highly recommend finding just about any other way to deal with your anxiety. Perhaps it was for the purpose of this book, if I want to spin it in a positive manner. Equally possible is the fact that I am just that crazy. Either way, again, I would never advise this approach. It was dangerous, reckless, it took much longer than necessary to heal, and it was beyond torturous to those who loved me. It is how it happened though and I now know that I alone am enough. In fact, I got it tattooed on my wrist. "You alone are enough" so that forever I remember my journey and that I am ok, even if I'm alone.

When you begin to come out of the cloudiness, you realize everyone in your life loves you and you somehow serve an important purpose. Once you realize this and trust in it, you will start to shift your mind. Your energy will be spent differently. You stop thinking others are better without you, because for once you believe they're not. They know you're better than that, and they know you're bound for something great. This is why they don't give up on you. And them not giving up is because they believe in you. Upon learning this we can begin to wonder why we don't then believe in ourselves. We eventually learn to follow their actions. We learn playing the victim is rarely healthy, even when you are the victim. It does not end well to stay in that space. Mourn, heal, do what you need to do but get out of that space as fast as you healthfully can.

When you know what the devil's voice sounds like, that is never ok. We have to learn to not run from this voice. We have to learn instead to be louder than it, and to one day realize it can speak, but it can't actually touch us. Its mental manipulation can cause us to physically react but that is still our choice in the end. We have to choose ignorance. It's one time in life where being ignorant is a must. We are empaths to the point where we can even feel sorry for the bad guys, so it's hard to set healthy boundaries, even against something that's hurting us. To not blame ourselves for something that is a part of us and inside us is so conflicting that it will drive us to a whole other level of insanity and crawling out from these layers is exhausting. That is the devil's hope though — to exhaust us so we can't get unburied and out of the coffin. But we learn we have to keep digging out and keep brushing it off. Once we get out, we're usually slammed with a mountain of reality and we can begin to feel faulted again. Now we're in the real world and a new life begins. One that can be terrifyingly new. This pattern of removing layers and being scared of what it will reveal will continue to happen. Over time, we learn to embrace these challenges and can even almost anticipate them, knowing each new one signifies we are still moving forward.

Like me, it could take you 30 years too, to figure it all out. Trust me, I'm still uncovering layers and I still fall backwards from time to time in failure, but my hopes in you reading this is that together we can alleviate and lesson some of the suffering you're dealing with daily.

Life is always going to be hard. Even when you find relief, start to have a "normal" life, or even finally figure out your passion and calling on Earth, it's not like all the doors open and it's smooth sailing. It's still tough and is difficult as all hell. That's what makes it worth it though. Being able to look back and see how far you have come from even just the day before is elating.

Your body has to put up with your wild mind every day. So, if all you can be grateful for at night is the fact that you survived the day, that is ok. At least take a moment to thank your body for not giving up on your mind. Thank your mind for not giving up on your soul, and thank your soul for wanting to find a way out and for knowing it's just a maze that you eventually figure out if you just open your eyes. **Open your eyes. We are only meant to think we know everything. In reality, we know nothing.**

Chapter 2

Self-Love

<u>What it is and my thoughts on it:</u>

Self-Love to me is essential and necessary. It is exactly what it says which is the act of loving one's self. If you can't love yourself, who can you love? If you can't love yourself fully, then how can you expect, fairly, for anyone else to fully love you? You are showing the world what you think of yourself and how you rate your self-worth. When people see how you see yourself, they're going to believe you and then yet we fault others for not loving us. We might say, "Why don't you love me?" to someone. Well, maybe someone once in a while needs to shout back, "Because you don't even love yourself so why should I?" just to see how fast things get quiet.

Love yourself first and trust that others will follow. Set the bar high and others will rise to it; those that don't want to or can't will only make room for those who want to and who can.

<u>Why I think it works:</u>

This works for me because anything that is loved is going to thrive and live a better life. Children, pets or even a house plant will survive and flourish if you take the time to love it. Why do you think you're any different? Why do you think you deserve less? We as humans tend to dismiss ourselves because we are the one who has to deal with the repercussions. We are the only one who has to live with the discomfort of being unhealthy 24/7. So, if we can "handle it," then we do and that's how we end up putting ourselves last. This has to stop. The whole "fill your cup first," and to "put your breathing mask on first," is all said for a reason. You can help someone else when you are half-full; however, imagine how effectively you could help them if your glass was full. Fully well, present, and healthy. Now, just as much as you think they deserve your best, why would you ever short-change yourself the very best of you? Snap out of it and start taking your life back, for yourself.

How I do it:

This is a huge piece of the wellness puzzle for me. I do everything from epsom salt baths, meditation, essential oils and walks outside, to shopping sprees, painting my nails, dyeing my hair or treating myself to a movie or some other kind of escape. I allow myself to be happy and not feel guilty about how I do it. I smile and don't question, "Why am I smiling?" anymore. Now, I just smile. I do what I want, when I want and if anyone conflicts with it, I explain, "I'm living my life and I'm doing this for me. It is a necessary step and process I'm going through and I would like some respect and space in this area." Lots of people may not understand, but it's not their place and if they truly knew what and why you were doing this, trust me, they would have your back, even if those words are never actually spoken.

Variations:

Music, listening to or playing an instrument, painting, spa treatments, massages, weight-lifting, cardio exercise, running, playing sports, and a million other activities and hobbies all apply here. This is really about what makes you happy and there is nothing off limits or too small to count in this category.

If it makes you happy, do it; if it makes you smile, keep doing it.

Ways to build it into your routine:

Just start. Start with one thing like a bath soak for 10 min. If you can't give yourself 10 min out of the whole day then we have bigger issues at hand. Right before bed take 3 min to wind down and meditate. While you're watching TV, doodle, journal or even grab some lotion and massage your feet. Literally, nothing is too big, nothing is too small. Be realistic with what you can schedule each day. This will help make it more sustainable as well as easier to maintain every day and build it up. **In my opinion, this is the most important because once you have a great foundation of self-love, all of these other methods we discuss will have that much more power when you bring them into play.**

Chapter 3

Self-Care

What it is and my thoughts on it:

Self-Care is very similar to, and can often be confused with, self-love. To me, the difference here is what you can see and what you can't. Self-care is you taking care of everything you can see whether it be your physical body, your home, your office space, your finances or even staying organized. All of this represents you taking care of yourself but leaves out what we can't see. Taking care of the mental, emotional and spiritual side is where you would go back to the self-love techniques and doing things that make you happy and fulfilled. Some of the things you do will fall into both categories. Honestly it's not crucial to distinguish them, just be sure to do them.

Why I think it works:

Just as the definitions are very similar and some could say interchangeable, so are the reasons why they work. Let's be obvious here. When you take care of something, it is going to thrive. We take care of each other and then often fall short when it comes to taking care of ourselves. Can you imagine if you allowed yourself to just shut that out a little so you could focus on you and give yourself some hard core care and love? Now imagine doing that for an entire day, week, month or even an entire year — just focusing on you, if you're single and don't have kids and can, or at least focusing more on you, for those of you who do have a spouse and/or children. Are you already making excuses? Well, stop, and let yourself have this. Everyone in your life will benefit from you elevating yourself to the best version possible. You, your partner, your kids, friends and family, co-workers and even strangers. Everyone benefits, especially you. In life, if you ignore something or perform poorly, then be prepared to constantly be trying to revive it or keep it afloat. Instead, what if you just took a little bit of extra time each day to tend to this being that is yourself. All of those extra minutes would start to add up and begin transforming you into a stronger mind and body. **The universe will not allow you to fall when you're truly trying to better yourself. If it does, just make sure you get up and try again. More times than not, it's because there is a lesson to be learned still. Look for it and when you find it, apply it.**

How I do it:

My routine definitely includes something every single day. My self-care is very "juvenile" in the sense that the average person might see it as not being substantial enough to include on this list but for me, every single thing you do counts! Don't discredit any method until you've really tried it. You dismissing the idea of it is just your anxiety once again winning. If all you did that day was make your bed then hats off to you! My list, you guessed it, includes making my bed, being sure to floss, brush my hair, take either a shower or an epsom salt bath, doing some form of cleaning or cooking and even a couple walks outside with my dog. Depending on the day I'll add in some meditation, essential oils or something of the like. **I make sure by the end of the day I've done a handful of things that are solely focused on me, my health, or my home.** No excuses with this technique because some things take up such a small block of time. After you start seeing and feeling results and knowing the benefits of these practices it makes it much easier to push through and stay committed.

Variations:

This is another one where the sky's the limit and only you know what will make you feel better. It could be physical like working out or going for a swim or tending to your space like cleaning an area of your home, organizing a desk, tossing old clothing away, cooking that recipe you've been dying to try or overhauling your diet and eating habits in general. Nutrition and what we put into our bodies has a large effect on our minds and even the slightest change can make a difference. Really anything goes here as long as you are recognizing that what you are doing is for you alone and it is something that is benefiting your health, your space or overall well being.

How to build it into your routine:

With each technique in this book I'm going to tell you to "Start, no matter how small, just start," and I will say it each time to drive this point home. Starting small makes sure you start at all and it also makes it easier to stick to it when the task at hand is rather daunting. Some of these practices simply take a minute, others can take 20. Choose what you want that fits into your time frame that you are committing to and go off of how much time you have so that you don't set yourself up for failure. Don't hit the ground running or do too much too fast or for too long. This can be a recipe for self-sabotage and frustration beyond belief. If this does happen however, get up and please start again. I've fallen behind dozens of times, but like working out you just get back into the rhythm as soon as you can. Pick up right where you left off and don't give yourself too hard of a time for letting your grip slip. You're human and you have one hell of an army you're fighting so it's natural to have some setbacks.

Chapter 4

Gratitude Journal

<u>What it is and my thoughts on it:</u>

I have yet to come across anyone who has kept a gratitude journal for a significant amount of time who will say anything negative about what it has done to their life. This says a lot. I, like most of us with chronic anxiety, still was skeptical. If I was going to keep true to myself though in genuinely trying to beat this thing, I had to give everything a try for at least a month. That was my deal with myself. This was how I allowed myself to not feel chained to these "tasks" or from mentally making them out to be chores. I tricked myself into thinking they were my idea and that I could abandon them at any time, after the first trial-and-error month of course. By week two, I was beyond pleasantly surprised to find that I was quickly becoming one of those cheerleaders for this methodology.

<u>Why I think it works:</u>

The power of the mind is an ever illusive thing that sometimes we just don't give enough credit to. The power of your thoughts is often underrated or dismissed. If you constantly think negatively, you're going to be negative, depressed or angered easily. If you think positively, the opposite will happen. However, it is not that black and white. This doesn't mean thinking positive will make your whole life all sunshine and rainbows and nothing bad will ever happen to you again. It simply means that you will spend less of your time dwelling in thoughts and spinning them into things that aren't even real or there. It helps you to be kind to others and expel good instead of freaking out over the tiniest of insignificant setbacks. Focus on the good and you will start to notice more of it. This isn't changing what's there, it's a matter of just opening your eyes and choosing what you see. It's almost like an optical illusion. Every single time you look at something or experience something you can have a positive reaction or a negative one. If you constantly make an effort to choose the positive one then you will naturally be happier. It isn't always the easier choice and sometimes you have to look harder at the illusion, but that is what makes it worth it. Actions speak louder than words and this instance is no different. You have to act on it. Even if in the beginning it seems forced, because lets face it, it will be, one day if you stick to it and trust the process I can tell you that the odds of slowly taking back control of your happiness are definitely in your favor.

We have the ability to retrain our brains and make new memories as well as let go of old ones. Imagine if the only memories you could hold onto were positive ones. While that is nearly impossible, we can attempt to alter most of them. Especially those that we ever so famously like to fabricate, exaggerate or make worse so we somehow feel better, justified in our emotions, and therefore validated in our sadness.

How I do it:

Each and every night I do this practice. No matter how tired I am and even if it is just one sentence I manage to write something, anything. I keep it in my bedroom and just as I brush my teeth it has become a part of my nightly routine. Often times I can't stop writing because so much has happened that day, while other days I have to pause for a few moments just so I can think of something at all. **Every day isn't perfect** and it never will be, but every single day there is at least one thing to be grateful for. Even if it's the breath in your lungs, there is something. **Find it, highlight it and give it the thanks it deserves. Celebrate that you even had a day to experience and end on a good note.**

Variations:

Any type of journaling can help. It sounds awfully cliché but I have learned in life that clichés exist because they have worked to a significant level of success for a significant number of people in the past. Clichés are often painted as a bad thing and I'm not sure why but I digress. Just like the rest, you can write as little or as much just be sure to write something so it doesn't go unnoticed. Actually give it a dedicated time slot somewhere in the end of your day.

How to build it into your routine:

Put the journal somewhere you will see it each evening. On your nightstand, by the toothbrush, on the stairs up to your room or even on the bed. Somewhere where you will see it and know to take action. After a few days it will become routine and you can move it into a less exposed place. If you want to keep it private, then keep it in a private place and use a pen or something else in its place as your "reminder".

Chapter 5

Morning Journal

<u>What it is and my thoughts on it:</u>

A morning journal can be a tough one to adapt to; however, this was by far the fastest technique for me as far as noticing a positive difference and shift in my thoughts. It is one of the more specific tasks but just like the others is adjustable to your life and how much you want to do. A lot of anxiety can come from cyclical thinking. From obsessing over things that have happened already, trying to pick apart what was said, overanalyzing actions and making the worst of them, to obsessions over the future about anything and everything that could go wrong, any confrontations that can occur, and any hindering activities on the to-do list. This cyclical thinking is what gives some of us an insane memory bank and the ability to recite things exactly the same way over and over. This can be a nice talent to possess however it can easily turn crippling. All that time the mind wastes recycling thoughts could be spent on making new memories or just, lest we forbid, enjoying the current moment in the here and now. This journal allows all of the conscious and sub-conscious thoughts to get out of your head and onto a piece of paper to relieve your mind of some of the work. There is something to be said about thinking something, slowing down to write it out, and even more power given if these words are then said aloud. This step gives power to your thoughts, the ability to change them around or re-frame them, and establish what it is that you want. It's also a time to discard thoughts that don't serve you or can disrupt the productivity of the day by lingering around in the dust in our minds.

Once this task is done the amount of free space available in your mind is unimaginable. The first thing I noticed was the ability to daydream. To really almost lose time for a minute or two and just daze off was a foreign and euphoric thing for me to experience. The lightness that I felt in both my mind and body was unreal. When people talk about how your thoughts can weigh or boggle you down, it really is a thing. I became free of my thoughts and became incredibly focused and centered. **This practice can be fine-tuned, yet even the rusty version reveals a new level of clear-headedness that should not be taken for granted.**

Why I think it works:

I can't help but think this activity can be compared to sweeping out your brain each morning. I imagine after an entire night of sleep the brain is so scattered from crazy dreams and a little offset that we need something to get the train back on the tracks after our feet hit the floor. For some people, this is why they think they need coffee each morning. That can be good for a physical boost and for some it's even how they "stay regular," but why not treat the brain a little differently and offer it a boost as well. This is exactly what this activity does. It takes out that trash that is the randomness of the morning and tosses out any unnecessary clutter so that the thoughts that belong there can move about more fluidly and not have such an obstacle course to master to get the attention and focus they need throughout the day.

How I do it:

This is best done first thing in the morning before even getting out of bed however for people with kids or even a dog, there's not always that luxury of having even 2 minutes alone when first waking up. Therefore, the activity can be pushed back just a little to once the morning routine is done.

I still make it a part of my morning I just shifted its time slot from first thing when I wake up to more towards the end of my routine. This is only a twenty minute difference and I can still feel the benefits. The effect might not be as prominent but it's good enough for me and it's honestly better than nothing. **With these activities I take what I can get and I don't beat myself up anymore about lacking absolute perfection.** Yes, you can one day be able to say this phrase too.

The formula for this journal is to begin writing basically as soon as your eyes are open. Wake up, roll over and grab that journal. First thing you write about is whatever you are recalling from the night's dreams. This will be a bunch of gibberish and will most likely not make sense but just write whatever you remember, even if it's illegible. This entire journal is about spitting out what is running through your mind in whatever order it occurs in your mind. No matter the thought, order, or sense of it, you write it down not even really paying attention to what you're writing because you are so focused on what is spewing out of your brain next.

Keep writing until the dreams fade and whenever that pause hits, move to phase two. This is simple, write three things you are grateful for that happened yesterday. This is a pleasant way to instantly shock your brain into realizing that no matter how badly you don't want to get out of bed you have good things in your life.

Then it's phase three. Here you just rant, rave, exclaim, complain, whatever your little mind desires. Nothing here is off limits. If you are ever allowed to be negative towards yourself or anyone else, now is the time. If we're being realistic there is no such thing as a human who never ever has an impure thought. It's just not possible nor is it in our genetic makeup. These thoughts do not make you evil or a bad person. It's what you do with these thoughts that dictates that. So here is your dedicated time and place to release them. Release whatever is angering you about the day before or the days ahead. That thing your boss said or whatever you think about that person you're feuding with. Let it all out and be honest. Don't skip a single thought because you think it's too harsh or mean. This journal can end up shredded, ripped apart or even burned to ash so write as if no one will ever read it because guess what? — If you don't want anyone to read it, you just destroy it once the activity is over. Write your heart and mind out onto that paper until you naturally stop. This can be a single page or ten, whatever you need to get out of that head. Once you're done, do whatever you want with it. You don't even need to ever read it. I've found it's better if you don't go back and read it because then it could put the thoughts back into your mind and then you've just negated the entire process. This exercise is meant to solely get those things out of your mind and gone for the day so once they're out you can dismiss them with more ease if they try to re-enter your mind during the day, but you just might be surprised at the lack of this happening.

Variations:

If your mornings are too crazy you can try doing this sometime midday; however, since the basis is clearing your mind first thing I would aim to follow those instructions. I will say again that any form of journaling I will always support so if all you can get is midday than go for it. You can try to write poetry or songs or even just writing random words and phrases. Getting stuff out of your head is an amazing feeling and you can even have journals everywhere of all different types. The act of taking something out of your head and putting it on paper so you can move on with your thoughts is extremely effective and helpful. If you live with people take a moment to ask them to respect your privacy and if they ever see one to just let it be. Or keep them in a private place. **I want to stress here that the level of honestly in what you write will equate the level of success you have with this technique.** In that sense do whatever you need to do to ensure you can be brutally honest in what you're writing because there is no fear of someone seeing or reading it.

How to build it into your routine:

Very similar to the gratitude journal keep the actual journal or a pen — something symbolizing the journal — somewhere you will see it each morning. For example, by your toothbrush, in the closet, by the coffee maker, by the TV remote, or anywhere else you would see it each morning will suffice. Dedicate any time in the morning that you have to it. If you only have a minute, it's better than nothing, but know that with this technique, around five minutes will yield the best results. Once you do this for some time just like the gratitude journal it will become habit and just a part of your routine to the point where you'll even begin to look forward to it.

Chapter 6

Meditation

<u>What it is and my thoughts on it:</u>

Meditation has been long recognized as a way to combat anxiety, depression, sleep deprivation and other medical issues. There have been studies performed on it's effects on the brain and everyone who practices it consistently swears by it. The only negative things I have ever heard were that, "it was too hard," or "it just didn't work for me" or "I had so much trouble focusing," all to which I would say, "it sounds like you didn't try hard enough" or "sounds to me like you gave up a little too soon." In situations like this I often ask the person how long they attempted this practice and to mimic their techniques, only to find out they barely gave it an honest attempt. Trust me, I know because I used to do the same. I would get frustrated with techniques or say that they didn't work for me but then I realized that was my anxiety once again speaking, and that if I truly looked at my efforts, they were poor at best. That is part of the reason I set out on this journey. To go back and give a fair shot at each of the remedies I had tried in the past as well as some new ones.

Meditation has so many alterations and ways to do it that it's kind of hard to mess up; however, there are proper and more effective ways to perform this practice. My overall opinion of it is that it is amazing if you give it half a chance. I always had my opinions of it and then I realized that part of me was shunning it just because that's what I do. My natural reaction to quite literally everything and anything that I don't know, is to shy away. If I think it'll help me, I shy away even more. Sounds self-destructive, no? I'll give you one guess as to what another symptom of anxiety is.

Why I think it works:

The human mind is so busy these days and technology has us all living in an environment where instant gratification is a must and thus daily let downs are a guarantee. We walk faster, we talk faster, we work faster, think and process things faster so naturally we probably even breathe a little faster. Meditation forces you to slow it down. Slow down the breath, slow down the mind and really let your body fall into place together the way a marching band would march and beat all to the same step and timing. **Meditation helps your body, mind and organs get in line and work together with synchronicity.**

What's the first thing someone says when someone is not ok? "Take a deep breath." It's common knowledge and makes sense as to why this works. Just as your blood needs to keep pumping so does your oxygen. Taking a deep breath forces you to pause, even if for just a second, and just think and be. Getting oxygen to the brain and organs can help calm you down and help your heart rate slow down and fall back into a healthy rhythm. As little as a couple minutes can help you. Even if you don't feel something right away, because sometimes you won't, trust that it is doing something on a subconscious level. Intense results depend on you and how serious you take it, but the subconscious and physical body will almost always be affected regardless. Keep up the practice and you will notice a difference after some time. Have confidence and keep going. This technique can take a little longer but the good thing is it does make you feel extremely relaxed once you get there. During the transition process, just know while you may not be able to tell immediately, you are bettering yourself and your body and what you're doing most certainly can't be hurting you, so why stop?

How I do it:

I start with however much time I have. I like to do it before and after physical tasks sending love to my areas of pain. Doing this practice beforehand I would compare to stretching before a workout whereas the after session works the same way a cool down does for your muscles after an exercise. This is basically a workout for your brain and heart, and the benefits can be both physical and mental. Remember you are rebuilding your practices to now include mental sides and not just physical sides. This is a prime example of how it can be comparable and although there are physical benefits the primary focus here is gaining mental health.

Variations:

Every meditation can be different. The duration can vary as can the pose you sit in. Your breath counts can vary as can the words you focus on. Some use colors to focus on while others use numbers. There can be different time frames for the breath and for the overall experience. Find one that works for you and stick to it until you feel comfortable adding a new one. Keep an open mind and try new things. Basically be creative. The only thing to steer clear of, is don't set an alarm to end your session. Come out of it naturally. When you want to be done, wrap it up and be done with it. You can start to look at the clock though before and after the session to get an idea of how long you are meditating to see if you need to adjust. For instance, the first time you might think you've been sitting there for five minutes and come to find only a minute has gone by. That's fine, just know that with time the opposite will happen. All of a sudden you'll be so relaxed that twenty minutes will fly by just like that. You'll be a pro.

How to build it into your routine:

Like everything else, start small and build up. Start with just a minute. Sounds silly right? But wholeheartedly, that one minute of meditation every day for 1 week is going to be more effective than doing a ten minute session only once a week. Consistency here is crucial. The more you practice the better you'll get at it. If you can only focus for two minutes, then only do two minutes. Don't force yourself to sit there for another eight minutes not actually meditating just so you can say, "I meditated for ten minutes today." It's not an easy thing, especially if you have a mental illness. Be honest with yourself and start small knowing that no amount is too small and even the shortest chunk of time will start to build a great chain reaction of results. This is a growing process. **Each time you meditate you are adding to the foundation that will become your practice of this technique. It will eventually come to you naturally. It may take time, but it will show up as long as you do.**

Chapter 7

Essential Oils

<u>What it is and my thoughts on it:</u>

Essential oils are just what they sound like. They are the oils gathered from specific plants in concentrated form that can possibly have great effects on certain conditions and symptoms. Before I go further, note that oils can be dangerous. If you have an unknown allergy or sensitivity to a plant and use that oil, a reaction absolutely will occur. When using on your skin always be sure to use a carrier oil such as olive or coconut oil to dilute these extremely potent oils. Also, do not get the terms "essential oil" and "extract" mixed up. The latter is often used in cooking or baking, and the former is usually just used topically or diffused in the air around you. Essential oils can be used as well in cooking, but you absolutely need to know what you're doing. I haven't even experimented with ingesting them, so I won't have any further advice in that area since I haven't explored it myself. If you want to try them this way then please be sure to do some research on them first or seek an expert before experimenting as they can be very dangerous if ingested incorrectly.

<u>Why I think it works:</u>

The same way aspirin originally was derived from willow tree bark and other medicines can come from plants, there is no reason to think that other plants can't have some medicinal properties too. As long as you're careful and use a carrier oil and oils of good quality then what do you have to lose is my perspective. You apply the oil and it either works or it doesn't.

This technique takes seconds so it is fast enough where it doesn't interfere with the day and thus makes it very easy to incorporate.

How I do it:

I dab a mixture on my wrists, temples, inner elbows and even my neck as well as sore spots on my back. Certain oils I put on my feet and give myself a little massage and sometimes I just need to take in a couple deep breaths of it for an effect. I also will dilute them in a spray bottle with water and just spray it around my house as an air freshener and bug deterrent. I use them in the laundry for an extra scent boost and other times they're in the epsom salt baths I take for added fragrant notes of relaxation. Another good investment can be a diffuser so even when you're sleeping the oils can be going to work calming you before you even wake up. Yes, I get sneaky with my treatments whenever I can.

Variations:

Don't like the concept of essential oils? Try another form of a scent such as a candle, fresh flowers or even potpourri. Our sense of smell is the sense closest tied to memory, so just as they can bring back sad memories they can absolutely bring back happy memories. Think of smelling that beach towel and reminiscing of the vacation you just took, or like they do in the movies, smelling the shirt of a loved one that you are missing. It's all the same as far as what it's doing to the mind so find what you like and surround yourself with these scents.

How to build it into your routine:

I keep some that I use less frequently in a drawer, and others I keep out next to my jewelry. I put on my watch, I put on a dab of oil. Brush my hair, put on a dab. I even keep a small bottle in the laundry room so when I'm washing my sheets I can put some drops in without having to go get them. I beat my laziness to the punch whenever I can so I have no more excuses as to why I'm not participating and at least trying. I have come to grips with the level of crazy that is myself and as long as it works, I don't care how I have to get it done. **This sense of freedom from my worries is an amazing feeling to reach and it was all done with these techniques so even when you're doubting them, I beg you to find a way to keep pushing forward.**

Chapter 8

Acupressure

<u>What it is and my thoughts on it:</u>

There are points on our bodies called pressure points. You can search for whole charts of the human body exposing each point as well as what applying pressure can do to it. Acupressure is that simple. You apply firm, fixated pressure to a point correlating to your ailment for a significant amount of time. I believe the average is five minutes. I'm fond of probably the most well known one that is located between your thumb and first finger.

Most of these points can have a vague description as to where exactly they are; however, when you're applying pressure you'll know exactly when you're on it because they hurt a little. Not in a way that's painful, but in a way you'll know you found the right spot. Once you've located it you simply keep the pressure firm and fixed and then just watch the clock.

I tend to use the one between the thumb and first finger because it is supposed to release stress, reduce anxiety and can be a tension headache alleviator as well. This can be hit or miss for me. Sometimes it works like a charm and other times I'm not so sure. I know it does something but I think it's more or less depending on how severe my symptoms are. In nervous situations this remedy does help, however in a full blown panic attack, it will most likely be a waste of time. **That's just the thing though, we are all different so what might not be a powerhouse tool for me might be your strongest go-to, so don't dismiss anything that isn't my number one just**

because for me it isn't the most effective. You have to be willing to try everything for yourself to find out what works for you.

Think of this as putting your mind through a science experiment where first prize is relief. I only attempted acupressure as a rescue method so perhaps if I were to push on this pressure point every day, even when it wasn't needed, it might have had a faster response time when I used it. I have a mat that I use daily for my back and save the more specific points for when I have a specific ailment. There are dozens of points on the body so it's hard to try them all at once.

Why I think it works:

When we get stressed we build tension. Our muscles tighten up and so do the rest of our insides. Just as you would go to a masseuse to get some knots worked out of your tense back and neck with firm pressure, the same idea is applied here. You are applying fixed and firm pressure to a specific area to release tension and allow parts of your body that correlate to these points to relax and release some tension.

How I do it:

You can go see a professional for this and get an entire body treatment or you can simply search for certain trigger spots and do self-treatments pretty much wherever you want. I personally opted to buy my own acupressure mat that came with a headrest. All I did was search online to find one that I liked and one that came with a headrest — to get my neck points — and there was plenty to choose from. They are all very similar, it's more or less about how many "points" you want on the mat that press onto your body. Whenever I want I take it out and lay on it for about 10 minutes depending on my day. I try to max this one out because sometimes it works so well, I feel like I could fall asleep. This would be a great practice to put towards the end of your day when you need to unwind before bed.

Variations:

Acupressure is acupressure, there really is no other version except there can be a similarity with acupuncture which is our next chapter. So we will get to that.

How to build it into your routine:

Just like with the rest, start small. Schedule an appointment with a professional or set an "appointment" time at your home. Use the mat as instructed and just like the others, consistency can be key here. You're not going to lay on it once and be cured of everything. **Stick with it, even if you don't see immediate results. Give the practice time to work, give your body time to react, and give your mind time to adjust to this new treatment.**

Chapter 9

Acupuncture

<u>What it is and my thoughts on it:</u>

Acupuncture is the ancient Chinese practice of sticking really small, thin needles in your skin, hitting pressure points and letting that trigger a release, relaxing you and calming your muscles. There are two forms of acupuncture to my knowledge — American and traditional Chinese practices. For me personally, the American version didn't do anything whereas the Chinese practice practically knocked me out cold. The first time I ever had a session using this practice, I fell asleep about halfway through and I woke up when they were re-entering the room when my time was up. Sounds crazy right? Well, it was crazy, crazy good that is. I had been knocked out cold and I had been drooling through the face hole of the massage table. It was kind of embarrassing, but I just said out loud, "That was amazing." Then when I left, I had to sit in my car for 10 minutes to let my head balance out before I felt comfortable driving. The treatment was so effective for me I knew there had to be a downside, and there was. The results don't last very long. Sometimes by the next day or two, it had worn off. At one point I was going three times a week which was extremely effective but then you have to begin to evaluate cost. You have to pick and choose with this one. Acupuncture isn't viewed as a permanent fix to begin with so these results were very normal. If it works for you, you can absolutely focus solely on this and therefore save money on other methods which would cost money. For example, going to acupuncture three times a week might be cheaper than seeing a therapist once a week. I was initially bummed to know how good I could feel only to find out that there wasn't a way to maintain it forever; however, I quickly learned I can't think this way. Once again this is my negativity and anxiety driving the wheel. Now I use it as my goal. My bar that I set to achieve each day knowing how good I can feel and trying everything to get there.

Why I think it works:

I would imagine your muscles being tensed up all the time and the sudden shock and piercing of the needles stimulates it and causes a break in the tension, therefore relaxing the muscle that was once all knotted up. I believe this stimulation also brings blood to the area which is always a good thing to have steady blood flow in an area of injury or in need of attention. **It's almost as if the needle pops a balloon inside your body and all the inflammation, stress and tightness gets released with the popping and it all dissolves away. You then have until your body builds said inflammation back up to enjoy the freedom and the good feels.**

How I do it:

This needs to be done by a professional only. I would recommend trying both the American/modern and ancient Chinese practices to see if one works better than the other for you and go off of that. Just like any profession, find someone you like and build a relationship. The more you communicate what is going wrong the more efficiently they can attempt to help you.

Variations:

The same as with acupressure, there really is no variation however if you don't like needles, docs, or don't have the money for multiple appointments then resort to the acupressure method in the chapter prior to this one. If you have the luxury, you can absolutely do both. I didn't have any issues, but to be safe just inform your practitioner that you are practicing acupressure at home as well. Tell them what works and what doesn't and it'll give them a good starting point.

How to build it into your routine:

If this technique works for you trust me, you will opt out of everything else to make sure you attend these appointments. That's all I need to say.

Chapter 10

Mindfulness

<u>What it is and my thoughts on it:</u>

Mindfulness to me is the art of being present. **Mindfulness is staying in and living in every moment while being in a physically relaxed state so that your mind cannot entertain fear or anxiety. Fear and anxiety can't be active while your mind and body are in this true state of relaxation.** This physically relaxed state with our minds focused on all of our senses in their present actions is pure bliss. This is an amazing tool yet was probably the hardest for me to get good at and also was another one that took longer to see results from. That being said, the results, once they kicked in, were life changing. It was absolutely worth being patient for this one and waiting it out and sticking to it.

<u>Why I think it works:</u>

This one also has to do with the mind being occupied. When you are distracted you can't and don't think straight or clearly. So the opposite must be true right? When you are completely focused in the now, and only paying attention to what's going on in front of you, then all you have, is focus and clarity. This is a moment that is not hard to get to, but rather hard to stay in. Once you learn how to stay in it the benefits are endless. It's like a fixed state of euphoria. For all I know, it's how people without anxiety feel all the time, but for people with anxiety this feeling of a break in the chaos of the mind, is simply ecstasy.

How I do it:

Start small and with what can be referred to as a "body scan". Begin at the top of your head and work down to your toes. With each new body part you flex each muscle you can think of for a few seconds and then relax it. As soon as you relax that muscle or area, you can feel the tension release and some looseness setting in and in that moment you need to take the relaxation one step further. Go completely loose and jiggly like jelly and just kind of shake it off and let your arms fall where they fall and really feel the numbness that is stillness. Take a deep breath in the stillness before moving to the next area. Take a breath in with each flexion and then a breath out with each relaxation letting everything go with it. Each time let your breath also lose tension and rigidity.

With your head use your hands to massage your temples and flex your eyebrows and move your ears around. Then move to your neck muscles to shoulders and on the way down to the toes. As you move to your legs be sure you pop back up to the top half of your body and your head to make sure they have stayed relaxed. If they've tensed up already wiggle around quick to get them to fall back into place, then continue. Once you're done, your whole body will be relaxed, and in a state of stillness. This state of full relaxation is extremely therapeutic and can reap wonderful results if practiced regularly. When you're in this state your mind is blank and you can then focus on every little sound around you, you can focus on one color or thing without any thoughts entering your mind, you can feel each texture and surface with greater sensitivity and even your scent and taste senses wake up.

In the beginning, it can take five minutes or so to do a full body scan but with practice your body will learn what you are doing as you begin one, and the muscles will fall into place before you even get to that area of the body as if you have disciplined them. That's when you know you've nailed it. When a body scan takes less than one minute instead of five.

As you begin this practice you will most likely find parts of your body that you probably are clenching subconsciously. The constant letting go of these compulsions will help tremendously in removing subconscious anxiety and stress especially on the physical body. This practice can take a while to see benefits especially if you are as tightly wound up as I used to be. I used to clench my jaw so badly, where if you even touched the back of my jaw line where my neck is, it was so sore as if I had been punched or bruised there. I had no idea I was even doing this until I began these exercises and noticed that when I went to tighten those muscles that they were already taut. This realization was eye opening and made me search for more instances where I would do a scan and find that muscles were already tight on me. I realized quickly that this could easily have been a contributor to my lifetime of headaches and migraines. I also was quick to realize just how much of my everyday life I was spending tensed up in an unnecessary fashion.

One evening I was laying on the couch on my side with my head on a pillow. Then I remembered, "Keep doing your body scans," so I did one and went to start with my forehead and eyebrows. It was then that I realized my head wasn't even sitting on the pillow. In my mind I was relaxing on the couch watching a movie, where in reality, I was sitting there with a clenched jaw, flexed feet and a neck that was so constricted it had my head actually lifted almost off the pillow. Who does that?! Apparently I do, a person with anxiety so bad they can't even relax right and who didn't even know how bad it was. Once I started seeing little signs like these that exposed just how bad my anxiety was, I became so committed to these exercises in search of more things that I wasn't aware I was doing so I could put a stop to them. Now, I don't clench my jaw, my jawline is never tender and when I have my head on the pillow, my head is really on that pillow, sunken in and all.

Once I nailed the muscle relaxation part I started to notice everything around me. This was my senses kicking in. All of a sudden, the grass was literally greener and the breeze was more prominent. Food had more flavor and scents brought about positive vibes and warm sensations. When I touched something, I really felt it and when I was looking at something I was laser focused on only that object. This was what being present meant. This was appreciating life. This was peace.

<u>Variations:</u>

You can start from head to toe or toe to head, you can just do your arms or back or you can constantly do the full body scans. I would say because this was so effective, try it the way I played it out first before searching for a variation. If this technique doesn't do anything for you after one month then feel free to explore, but I firmly recommend the normal practice, and to do the full body scans in the beginning especially because you really don't know how bad you could be tensed up until you focus in on each body part multiple times a day.

I would do a full body scan, get relaxed and then continue with my activities for the day, and then not even five minutes later, I would do a scan and find out I was already back to tightened up, head to toe. This was a long and daunting process for me, but it was only long because I had so much to unwind.

I will say that from a different perspective, it does actually work fast because each time I went to do a scan, I was able to get relaxed quicker and quicker each time. I also found the level of tenseness was less each time around. Just a touch less, but enough for me to notice a difference. Then one day I went to do a scan five minutes later and all of a sudden, I was still good! I didn't need to do another scan! I was able to maintain relaxation for the entirety of the five minutes. It starts small, like all of these do, but it builds and builds and ends up changing something in you and in your mind. Just like how my idea of happiness was skewed and altered, well so was my idea of "being relaxed". Having knowledge of what those feelings are actually supposed to feel like helps me build a new norm and makes my body and mind set the bar much higher so I know exactly where I can be each day so I'm not searching for that target or shooting blind each morning. I know where I can get to, I know my possibility, I know what it's like now to feel good, I know how to get there, and how to stay there. I know what it feels like so I know not to stop until I've reached this state of mind and body. Make sense?

How to build it into your routine:

This one is fantastic because you can do it almost anywhere. Especially when you get really good at it and even make up your own body scan "shortcuts". Then you can be in the grocery store and do a quick scan in the middle of the aisle to kind of check your muscles into a less rigid state. This is a great one to pair up with meditation. If you sit down for a meditation session and you find you're constantly having trouble focusing or responding then try some mindfulness first. Sit down as if to meditate and start with a body scan. Start from your head and work down to your feet and focus on each area. Flex, relax, and go one level deeper than relaxed before moving onto the next area. By the time you're done you will be in a full state of relaxation that is comparable — if not almost exact — to how you need to feel during meditation. Again, your senses will awaken and things will feel, smell, taste, sound and visually be more stimulating. So when you reach this moment you can stop and get up, or you can dive one level deeper and take it into a meditation session by keeping your body fully relaxed and bringing your breathing to the forefront and focusing your mind on the breath and staying relaxed. This is a great introduction into meditation if you are struggling.

Chapter 11

Yoga

<u>What it is and my thoughts on it:</u>

Yoga is the practice of making slow and precise movements of your body into specific poses that you then hold for a significant amount of time helping the body to tone and strengthen muscles while improving flexibility. Some yoga can be very basic and simple and some poses are incredibly difficult and need an expert or sometimes several months of practice to perform them correctly. I like yoga and wish I could focus better to perform these exercises better. Whether or not you have anxiety, sometimes the body responds better to exercises like tai-chi, qi-gong, pilates and yoga that are based around steady, slow and focused movements. Other times our bodies can need hard-core cardio and weight training. It all depends on you and what your body and more importantly your mind responds to. The beauty of this exercise is that there is zero experience needed to start. There is beginner's yoga and even gentle yoga for those who need to start super simple and work their way up. This again is an example of quality vs. quantity. You don't necessarily need to be throwing weights around to gain results. Smaller efforts can be more effective sometimes and other times they're not. It can change around a bit. **This is why you need to listen to your body and mind. Sometimes it will want cardio and other times you just need to do some yoga.**

Why I think it works:

This form of exercise is all about form and precisely maneuvered poses. The level of dedication to your breath and movement is similar to some of the other methods in that in that moment, it's all about being present. You are centered and the rest of the noise goes away while you hover in this zone. Eliminating the surface distractions can help your mind and body get a break so that they can then work on getting rid of some of those subconscious distractions that we talked about that we aren't even aware of. **The more we stay present, the more time our subconscious has to clean up the mess that is in our minds and begin to declutter some of those unnecessary thoughts. The more our minds can find several ways to do this, the better our state of mental health and our well being will be over all.**

You can't do yoga all day every day, but you can do yoga for 20 minutes, then practice mindfulness while at your desk all day, then go home and lay on your acupressure mat, then move to an epsom salt bath with essential oils while you have candles lit and are blasting your favorite tunes before you brush your teeth, hop into bed and write in your journal. Do you see here how the techniques can begin to build up, cross over each other, and easily fit into your day? Each step is you working on your mind. They all come together and because you did yoga, your next step of mindfulness will be easier because you are already somewhat relaxed. Then when you lay on your acupressure mat you don't need to as long because the yoga and mindfulness have kept you so relaxed and so on and so on. It is an army and together they really work!

How I do it:

The easiest route for this is to take a class. I like this because then you're not concerned about whether or not you're doing it right. The other easy way is to go online and find tips, poses, and even videos of sessions. You can even buy a book with pictures of poses and to learn more about the history of this practice. As always, with going with a professional it adds a level of accountability that for some people is crucial in them achieving goals. Take a class, make a couple friends, and have it become a practice that you exude and are proud of. Trust me, you will find people who can relate and who even share some of your struggles. Every person who does yoga loves it and does it for different reasons however odds are you will find someone who uses it to combat anxiety. Start a conversation and see what else they do to combat anxiety. **Perhaps you'll learn something or perhaps they can learn from you, and that honestly is a gift they probably seek often, but rarely are given, so seize that moment and do good, pay it forward.**

Variations:

Pilates, qi-gong, and tai-chi are not necessarily direct variations but I find they fall into similar categories in the sense that it's not all about sweat, high heart rates, or throwing around weights. That again is beneficial for some people but for those who need a "calmer exercise" these are it.

How to build it into your routine:

Just make an appointment. Ask around to find someone you know who either does it already or who has been wanting to try it. Buddy up and go to a class. If it becomes too expensive to keep up with the classes then go out and buy your own mat and take mental notes in the class to then go home and do the same routine. Go home and turn on some music, and do it in the comfort of your own space. Be motivated enough to do this at home though and stick to your guns. Some people are not able to stay committed to an activity that they hold the power to. Meaning if it's up to you to do it, and it's not a class you pay for or are meeting someone at, it can be easy to put it off or cut it short when it's just you. Sometimes you'll need a little push, so find a way to do that and use it. **It is your most powerful tool if you can find this inner force to override your inner voice. Sounds complicated, and it is, but we're here to make it less complicated right? The effort and desire are already there, so let's put them into action.**

Chapter 12

Re-Framing

<u>What it is and my thoughts on it:</u>

Ok, I know I'm beginning to say this about a lot of these but this is one of the biggest ones for me. I mean, if I didn't have such success with all of these then I wouldn't waste my time, or yours, writing about them. They all, in their own right, have earned my respect.

If you have had anxiety for a long time, odds are that some of your memories aren't always the most pleasant. Even the pleasant ones this illness sometimes has an inclining to destroy by highlighting a negative or somehow finding something wrong with it. The goal of this is to reverse that. They say time heals all wounds. I don't necessarily agree with that. I believe re-framing can though.

Re-framing to me is something I like to call "flipping the script". Inside our heads is a movie of anything and everything we can ever remember about our lives. What this tool is meant to do is take that movie script and "flip it". Take it from a horror movie and make it a comedy, or romantic drama, with a happy ending of course. It's taking any thought you have whether past, current, or about the future, and re-working its wiring in your brain. This technique deals with taking any instance and looking at it as a puzzle with many pieces, and altering the way your mind sees each piece of this whole puzzle. Each part that is negative we either deal with and rid our minds of or we flip it to a positive thought. Needless to say this applies only to negative thoughts — why would you want to change any positive ones — and can work wonders on how you process things you experience daily.

Just as your mind can take positive things and find something awful to hone in on, we can take negative experiences and flip them to positive ones. Think of finding the diamond in the rough. Sometimes you really have to dig and other times it's right at the surface if you just take the time to look. We tend to not do this naturally because it goes against the grain of what we know as humans. Let's not mention it's also a little out of our comfort zone and it's more difficult then the alternative, so we naturally retract away from it. This technique, once you're adapted to it, can work wonders though. Picture finding the silver lining but multiplied. Again, this doesn't mean your life will be fantastic and negative emotions are now at bay. **Reframing simply brings truth to the fact that you cannot change or control what happens to you, but that you can absolutely control how you react to it as well as your actions that follow as far how you handle obstacles in the future.**

Why I think it works:

Part of this is you taking your power back. The feeling that you have control of how you respond to something is intensely rewarding and only leaves you wanting more. It is an addictive way of thinking and proves to be a strength when given the attention it needs.

Think of our minds as cluttered rooms with hidden gems like a scavenger hunt. Find and expose these hidden gems and you get an amazing rewarding feeling. Picture your past as a deep dark forest. Go into it not afraid of what you're going to find because you know you can always leave when you want. Go in looking for the good things and coming out with only them. Leave the dirt, leaves, and twigs behind and dig for the gold. There is plenty there, although it might take some time to find it. You might have to go pretty deep into the forest or you might have to just go to the edge but will then have to dig deep, but trust, something is there. Find it, hold onto it, and take it home and put it on the mantle. Show it off, make it the centerpiece of your home in your mind and build off that.

I know the metaphor gets a little deep there but read that last paragraph again if needed. I'll sum up with saying that basically picture your current mind as a house that you're always decorating with memories. Keep it tidy, and only decorate with the positive memories. **What you think of today is what you choose to think of from your past.** Only choose the good to decorate your home. When you walk into the forest that is your past, never come out with a negative. If you find one, that's fine but don't bring it home until you've dealt with it or found something positive about it.

Nothing here is too small, too insignificant, or undeserving of your attention. If you have a lot going on in your forest here is where a therapist will help. Don't go unpacking your whole life by yourself. Ask for help or someone to talk to. Revisiting some of these negatives can take a toll, but in the long run it can be extremely healthy and for some of us it is actually necessary to begin our healing. Have someone by your side in some capacity to help you through this should you begin to feel too much pressure or an overwhelming feeling from the negatives. I've been there, so it is most definitely a possibility you'll feel some heavy emotions, but the good side is that I have now dealt with a lot of my past and come to peace with so many things that I probably would've just kept buried. I had help along the way so don't be ashamed if you need it too. What you are doing is brave and not for the weak. It exudes strength that some don't have so show pride in your actions and really celebrate what you're doing for yourself. Your future self will thank you, I am sure of this.

How I do it:

I had to practice this every single day, almost every single second in the beginning. It used to take lots of focus but now it comes more easily and I find myself talking through something and "flipping the script" before I even have the time to let the negative thoughts creep in. Reaching this point and the feeling that your mind has adapted this methodology and when it becomes second nature is an incredible feeling that I hope one day you can experience too. It's amazing to feel that you can be happy. For me, it got to the point where I was convinced something was wrong with me. I'm not a hypochondriac, but my level of happiness changed so drastically in the beginning there were times it actually was really uncomfortable for me. I thought it was wrong to be so happy for absolutely no reason at all. Once it was bluntly told to me that I should never question happiness and that I wasn't manic, I was able to adjust. Yes, that's how crazy some of us are. We think happiness is something wrong with us. We're so used to chaos and drama that it becomes our home. So when we pick up our things and move to a new home, it's going to feel weird. A good weird, but weird like you're only on vacation and it isn't your new real home. This is tell tale that you know what you're doing is working. I had a therapist once express their sadness learning this of me to think that I had been so unhappy for my whole life that a little happiness made me so uncomfortable and actually scared me into thinking something was wrong.

I look back now and will always remember how the sadness felt only so that I can count my blessings and know how far I have come. I have to keep that feeling on a very small level and somewhat familiar so that I can recognize when it starts to try and creep back in. For that reason only, I hold onto it a little bit, otherwise it is mostly gone. When I feel the pulling backwards of my illness, is when I grab this technique the most.

Variations:

I call it flipping the script, but some may call it finding the silver lining, some just call it being positive. There isn't really another version besides just simply having a healthy rotation of your thoughts. As soon as a negative tries to come in, reject it and flip it to a positive. With this technique you want to watch your verbiage and start to speak more positively about everything. Even small things. The more you find a positive in everything you see, the more naturally this will become second nature to you. This takes effort in the beginning but once your mind adjusts it comes pretty easily.

How to build it into your routine:

Just Start! Like the rest, start somewhere. Pick one thing and find a way to flip it. Past, present, or a worry about the future, pick something and find a more positive way to view and think about it. Challenge yourself and take a 24-hour day, and see if you can go the whole time with only thinking positive thoughts, saying positive things to others, and only dwelling on positive memories. Practice makes perfect and just catch yourself and correct yourself and most importantly don't be embarrassed by how often you need to do this. For me it was every minute. For some it might seem like every five minutes or even every second that a negative is trying to enter, and that's fine. This is about the fact that you are recognizing its appearance to begin with here, that is the first step. You take away so much of its power with exposure and taking the blindfolds off. **You're taking your life back, it is a process, and for it to take time is a definite. Strap on your patience and stay confident.**

Chapter 13

Medication

<u>What it is and my thoughts on it:</u>

Medication is self-explanatory; however, I have a lot to offer on my thoughts about it. I have experienced both ends of the spectrum when it comes to anti-anxiety medications. I have tried my fair share of different medicines for over a decade before finding one that worked. Most of them I had absolutely horrible side effects and reactions to, everything from nausea, headaches, and insomnia to full on hallucinations. Then there were those that made me way too tired. There were some that worked perfectly but aren't safe for long-term and others that just didn't work at all.

Once you find the right medicine, it can be heavenly. For some people they will turn a nose at medicine and for the most part, that is me too. I tried to be stubborn and prove I didn't need it, but then one day I would have a moment when a white coat would be telling me, "I know you don't like this but the alternative for you right now is not ideal, you need to give the medicine a chance otherwise this could end up killing you." You can only hear this a handful of times before you finally have a moment of vulnerability where you just give in. This is not giving up, but rather   accepting the fact that this just might be stronger than you and just might not ever go away on its own.

Anxiety isn't associated with being a deadly mental illness on its own. It is important to recognize though that the behaviors anxiety can induce can absolutely be slow, or even fast, killers.

When we are stressed we seek a vice, it is human nature. Some common examples can be smoking cigarettes, developing an eating disorder, self-harming/cutting, alcohol abuse, or prescription or street drugs. Any one of these can easily kill you, mix a few and your chances increase. This is when anxiety can become extremely dangerous and you may need to follow your best interest in seeking something more powerful to help you.

Medication should always come at the advice and supervision of a professional and one who is willing to work to find the right combination for you specifically. Having a doctor not pushing pills, but having a serious heart-to-heart and explaining your case, and how you may think you have a hold on this but you really don't, is sometimes a reality check that is much needed. For me it was not only needed, it probably saved my life.

Because of the terrible side effects I had experienced with prior medications, I was scared and scarred to try any more. I also had watched friends on their own trials of medication and knew I wasn't the only one struggling to find balance. Finally, while in therapy and realizing all the stuff I was digging up was going to inevitably make other things surface, I knew I needed something in my back pocket. I needed backup, a parachute. I agreed to try another medication with my doctor on the terms that the second I said, "No," he would move to the next one with zero hesitation or questions. I even listed a few side effects I'd be "willing to suffer" if it helped my anxiety. His response was, "How about we just find one where you have zero side effects. There's no reason for you to feel you need to deal with anything more than you already are." He picked up a thick book apparently full of different medications and information and said, "I have all the time in the world to find the right one for you." That blanket of security was probably the single most important thing any doctor has ever said to me. I had never felt so supported in my life. So, we started. The first medicine gave me flu-like symptoms after two days so we stopped. Then luckily that's where this new experiment ended. The next one would be my magic formula.

The main reason I became supportive of medication and finding one that worked for me was an extremely important one. It was because I have had this illness my entire life, so all I knew was chaos. The only voice I trusted inside was that of the devil. I had never truly slept nor knew what sleep was like. I had never experienced actual happiness. I experienced what I thought was happiness, and what others had described, but it always had a falseness to it, where it felt like an act or a mask I had to maintain to keep everyone fooled. This extra energy to keep this up was draining, beyond exhausting, and just all around unhealthy, but it's what I did because it was all I knew. My furthest memories include anxiety so how was I ever to truly achieve happiness when I had no clue what happiness felt like inside. You can't aim for something you can't see and you certainly can't exude a feeling you've never felt.

Sure, I had been happy at times like celebrations and other obvious life happenings but to be happy all the time or when I wanted to — I had no idea how to do that or feel that. I tried my hardest but at times, it was obvious I wasn't very good at faking an emotion that I didn't even trust was real. So many people are unhappy in the world, that I thought my pretending was just what people did. I didn't believe the people who said they were happy, that they slept at night, or that they didn't have negative thoughts all the time. I thought it was all a lie and my paranoia thought it was all a set-up. This is where the medicine basically saved me. It gave me the ability to feel inside what happiness is like. It gave me glasses so I could see the target I needed to hit each day as far as my mood, my positivity, and my thoughts. I finally got it. I understood just how good someone could feel with zero effort being put forth and for no reason at all. Can you imagine being happy "just because?" That was the eye-opening moment for me. It wasn't that all of these previous attempts at these techniques weren't working, it was that I didn't know the feeling I was striving for. It wasn't that I was doing them wrong, it's the feeling that I was aiming for that was wrong. I was aiming for my version of happiness, which wasn't happiness at all mind you, instead of aiming for true bliss. Once I had this feeling inside my mind and body, I knew how to take every single technique and tool in the box, go back, and re-try using them so I could see if I could get this feeling each time. That's how my venture started and my rear-view mirror is somewhere left behind in the dust at my starting line.

The bar had been set higher than I knew it could go and more importantly, I could hit it. Knowing I could hit it made me want to do just that. To wake up each day and do whatever techniques I had to do that day to hit the bar and stay there until the end of the day when I would sleep and then wake to do it all over again. That's just it for some of us — We just need something to help us feel how happy we can be, so we know what to strive for. For me, medication was necessary to get there and I'll never question anyone again who needs it. Some of you might not need it and these techniques alone will work for you. For those who do need medication, just know it's possibly worth the hell that can be finding the right one.

If I ever decide to come off my medicine, I'll always know the level of the bar. I know how I'm supposed to feel and therefore I know what to aim for. You have no idea how many bicep curls you can do with a five pound weight until you pick it up and experience it first hand. This first hand experience with happiness gave me the ability to fast-forward my progress and it helped all of my techniques begin to take action a little sooner because I knew what feelings to hone in on and which ones to dissolve. I finally had a clearer separation of what was the good and what was the bad trying to fool me into thinking it was good. I had a clarity of who the good voices were and who the bad ones were, as well as how to shut them up. I have learned that just like insulin or a birth control medication I would never knock someone for using, why in the world should I knock someone for this. I became accepting of it and more comfortable with it as the weeks past. I had zero side effects. It was an emotional process, a shedding of the old me, and I mourn her all the time. It's not that I miss being her, but rather the life and people I had in my life while I was her. It's the familiarity that is missed. Living outside your comfort zone can be hard sometimes. I always know I can go back to being her, but am very aware that is a deadly consideration. I look at my life now and often can't find anything wrong with it and in those moments I am proud to have been her and learned from her but I never want to be her again.

Your devils won't always go away through this process of healing and you will never forget their voices. They sound a lot like your own voice, like your best friend. Throughout this process I have learned to distinguish even the slightest comments and whispers from this voice though to keep myself on track. I have "shhh..." tattooed on the bridge of my neck and my right shoulder to tell this side of me to remain quiet and remind me that they are never to return. Sometimes they come knocking when I least expect it and sometimes I open the door; however, now it's with a chain across the top so they can't force their way in and with a sturdy "No, thanks" that I turn them away. This makes me sound crazy, but I don't care about how I'm viewed anymore. We all have voices. We all have a subconscious. Some of us just have ones that are a little louder and have less than healthy objectives for us. This doesn't mean we're weak and even if it does, So What? Recognizing that this was my reality and that there were plenty of others who were like me was all I needed to truly not care anymore if someone judged me or questioned me. In that ability alone I've healed tremendously. Know that in order to heal a wound, you need to admit the wound is there to begin with.

I'm ok with admitting that my chemistry needs a little extra work. Even more importantly noted, is that I'm ok with needing an arsenal of tricks and tools everyday to do this extra work. Acceptance is huge here and is such a necessary act to perform daily.

In my experience, as you begin to gain more control over your anxiety, you might find that you don't need as strong of a dose or maybe even any of the medication at all. If this begins to happen you will notice that the medication might start to have a different effect on you or you might begin to have side effects because it has now become a medication your body doesn't necessarily need anymore. Using a rough metaphor, let's examine and compare insulin and diabetes. Let's say you are a diabetic using insulin. You have to test your blood each time to know when you need it and how much. We can't do this with anxiety medication. It's a set dose whether we need that much or not every day. Let's say the same diabetic drastically altered their diet and daily routine and actually reversed their disease. Now, they don't need insulin injections at all. So, what do you think would happen to them if they kept injecting insulin daily without even checking their levels? They would have some serious side effects and it would have the possibility of turning quite ugly. Let me say from experience, anti-anxiety medications are no different in this sense. Even after months of being on it, be sure to always stay on track with your doctor/s and always have those close to you informed of what you're doing so they can tell you if and when something starts to seem off about you. Medications that mess with your mind and chemistry can be very tricky and when you're "in it," it is most definitely harder to notice if something is off about you. This is where your support team is crucial. Trust them and that they have your best interest in mind.

Why I think it works:

For some of us, we just have a chemical imbalance that needs correction. There are a lot of different medications and that's because we all are chemically different. What I believe happens or the way I feel it changed me is that it seemed to turn off some switches in my head while simultaneously turning some on that have never been on before. There is a newly lit home in my head and there's beefed-up security to keep out the bad guys.

When a panic attack comes forth, I can actually feel my mind switching certain parts of my brain off in a rush to stop the chain of reactions going on. This is a very hard and odd feeling to explain, but it's like it calms down my irrational voices and my logical and reasonable voices come forth. It's almost instant but not fast enough where I don't feel it happening. The only downside is sometimes it only goes that far. The physical side effects like my heart racing, pulse increase, blood pressure spike, vomiting, and hyper-ventilation can all still happen; however, the mind being controlled is the most important for me so I'm ok with that for now. It also is comforting to feel it when it's working because then I feel like the medicine hasn't changed me. It doesn't feel like it's working all the time, it really only kicks in when I need it to. Whether or not that's true I have no clue, I'm just going off of what and how I feel because it is what works for me. Sure, there is truth to the world, but every now and again I like to live in the grey areas and just believe whatever makes my heart happy. Some answers to life's mysteries we will never know. Instead of trying to figure them all out, now I make my own conclusions based on what is positive for my experience.

How I do it:

I take something time-released daily every morning and I have a secondary medication I take for breakthrough anxiety and when I have panic attacks. I see my doctors often for follow-ups and to keep track of my progress and that's about it. I do remind myself daily of the dangers of suddenly stopping these medications so I also know that whenever I want to try going without them, that a plan needs to be laid out first to do so.

Variations:

There are tons of different medications and I won't list specifics because of course they all need to be monitored and taken carefully, but your doctor can list what types of medication are suitable for you, as well as any other types of therapies you may be considering such as a psychologist or psychiatrist. It can take years to find the right one or combination so try your best to be patient and find a doctor who will be patient with you, as well as who will fight for you. Looking back, I didn't always have doctors who were fighting for me and therapists who believed in me. I'm here to tell you they exist. Find them and hold on to them!

How to build it into your routine:

This is self-explanatory as well, but to remember to take your medicine, you can set an alarm to remind you or put them next to your other medications, by your toothbrush, keys, phone, or other things you know you will definitely grab in the morning. If you already take medicine/supplements in the morning then just simply add to the list. If you are working with a doctor to find the medications that work for you, I recommend keeping a journal. Some of these medications, if you have side effects, you will want to monitor and keep track of them. This especially applies to the mental side effects. Tell others around you that you trust and who know you well, that you are trying new medications so that if they notice something about you is off, they can alert you. Not to scare you but some of these have side effects like mood changes and you might experience them without even knowing so the more people watching out for you the better. **For this process and transformation you need an army internally as well as externally. Build it with trust in mind and with only people who have your best interest at heart as well as a lot of patience.**

Chapter 14

Coloring, Drawing, and Painting

What it is and my thoughts on it:

Another that on the surface is self-explanatory, but we will take it to a deeper level. I never considered myself much of an artist in the sense that I wasn't a good drawer. I thought that one had to be talented in order to have a reason to draw or color. Once again, I couldn't be more wrong. Drawing, painting, or coloring can be extremely therapeutic. I don't care if it ends up being a huge pile of mixed paint that in your mind looks horrible, it is your masterpiece. It might not sell online or make you money, but what it can do to your mental health is priceless.

One thing I think we all can find beauty in is art. So if the end product is so amazing and soothing can you imagine the process to create it? You don't need to be any good at it — this can be like the journals where you can just toss the finished product — but it is important to open those creative channels in order to get them flowing so that creativity can be used in other facets as well. This simple task does just that and keeps these channels open as long as you keep acting on it.

Why I think it works:

I believe this works because it forces a part of the mind to open that anxiety likes to control and keep closed off. Our creative outlets are not necessary to live so-to-speak, so I feel like because they are so easy to turn off, our brain choses to do so because it needs that energy to fight this anxiety, or it puts it as a lower priority because we have so much other "important stuff" going on. Anxiety is a hoarder for time, energy, thoughts, and brain activity. This exercise forces that channel inside to open back up, even if just a little bit. That channel is what makes you you, and can have you feeling more like yourself and calmer at the same time, in no time. When you give attention and time to this side of your brain, guess who starts to get depleted? The anxiety side. The more the habit builds and the bigger it gets, the harder it will be for your anxiety to turn off this side of you, thus weakening it in the process.

<u>How I do it:</u>

If you want to go the thrifty route, buy one of those adult coloring books and a pack of crayons, markers, or colored pencils, whatever medium you prefer and get to it. It doesn't matter if you only start with a minute or literally only coloring a small circle for five seconds, just start and work your way up to however long you want given the time you have. This is something where it's important to do it every day though. If you don't feel like it, then just at least color one small block and then you can be done for the day, but commit to those five seconds. Eventually one day you will have a desire to color longer, go with this desire and see where it takes you.

Due to the need to save money I started with coloring and it worked so well I just stayed with it, but eventually I want to venture out to one of those painting classes they have everywhere. For now though, it's just an adult coloring book and some markers and coloring pencils so I can go off of what I feel that day. Sometimes I like bold colors and other days I like soft colors. Sometimes I color for 10 seconds and other times it's for 30 minutes while the TV is on in the background and I just zone out for a bit. Somedays I look forward to it and other days I despise it. This might sound weird, but after some time, some of these tools you might begin to resent, and that's completely normal in my opinion because it's not the actual action that I dislike. It's the fact that I need to do it.

Sometimes I wish I didn't have to do all these things to feel good. Then I remember how bad it could be, and that others are dealing with the same, if not worse, issues and that I should be grateful that I even have the ability, let alone option, to do something so easily that someone else might regard as a luxury. This is why I hold on to that glimmer of the old me. In these moments of almost being a brat, I remember who I used to be. I immediately "flip the script" and realize how bad things could be and am then grateful for how far I've come. In that moment I become aware that I'm confusing something for being annoying, with an understanding that it's just the anxiety talking. I have recognized that the happy me does want to do these things because they make me happy. The side of me that doesn't is the anxiety trying to sneak back in and guess who has to fight it, me. It boils down to the anxiety or the techniques and guess who rarely wins. Exactly.

Variations:

Anything art related. You could literally just scribble nonsense and there will be a connection made to this part of your brain. You can doodle, draw, paint, write poetry, write a song, sing to some tunes, or if you can afford it, learn to play an instrument. Anything here works as long as it doesn't really involve having any serious conversations or interactions with anyone and where you can truly let go and just be in the moment with the art. When you are in these moments remember your mindfulness and really just get lost in the process.

How to build it into your routine:

I leave mine out on the coffee table or counter so it's always there ready to be a part of my routine. Instead of magazines on your coffee table you can have coloring books with a fun tin full of markers and pencils. You can eventually find a spot for them less in the open, but in the meantime keep it somewhere you can see it so you can remember. You can even keep these with your journals and do it right before bed or in the morning for a minute while you're brushing your teeth if you're in a rush. Do it while you're waiting for the coffee maker or while waiting for water to boil for that pasta you're making for dinner. This one is an any-timer. Take advantage of that. You have five seconds to color a single block. Do it.

Chapter 15

Dancing

<u>What it is and my thoughts on it:</u>

Ah, dancing. Also very self-explanatory but needs a little guidance. There's a saying to "Dance as if no one is watching," and although it's unfortunate that the world judges us to the point where this is even a thing, it truly does hold meaning. To be able to do something while knowing you're not being judged is such a freeing feeling. Dancing is one technique that is full of self-expression and that can really just let you let it all out. To feel benefits from letting yourself be free of judgement, and to let your body do whatever it wants is a hard thing to explain. The commercials where someone is dancing in a field of flowers or while they're cooking or even cleaning seems silly but if you try it, you just might find yourself smiling amidst the activity. Try it now, just stand up and move your body however it wants to for ten seconds. Sit back down and see if you can't help but laugh at yourself or think in amazement at how awesome of a dancer you apparently are. Either way, imagine being able to create this feeling every day with just ten seconds of dancing. Not feeling it? Well, then dance longer until you do. Maybe you have more you have to get out. **Keep dancing until you forget what it was that your brain was so tied up in and then you'll see what I'm really talking about.** Trust me on this one. No one's watching so again, what do you have to lose?

<u>Why I think it works:</u>

I think this gives our minds a break. It's that simple. Sometimes people can move in silly ways that make us laugh and sometimes we are in awe at watching a dancer perform at seeing just what the body is capable of. To think you need to go to that extreme to get a sense of fulfillment would be silly. It's like the drawing or painting. We don't have to be an expert to get the same satisfaction of accomplishment or a little joy in our hearts. It's about what we need, how we feel, and what our body lets out when we give it an outlet. If you talk to most artists they are extremely humble about their talents and more or less just comment that they are happy they are able to make other people smile and that they love what they do. They might have studied on perfecting their art, but that by no means is a necessity to be able to feel good from doing it. Dancing or any movement can be underrated and the idea might even seem silly and make you want to immediately shy away from it, but just try it. Like the rest, start small and just try. What's the worst that can happen? Honestly. Plus us sufferers of anxiety need to learn to laugh at ourselves anyway. Not that I ever do, I'm an amazing dancer.

<u>How I do it:</u>

I just started dancing from the bedroom to the bathroom. It's that small and simple to begin. Then I would dance while folding laundry or a different chore even if it's just a little foot and hip movement. We're not talking ballet or tap here, although that's perfectly fine and kudos to you for going big and bold, but any movement will suffice. Just move your body. Pretty soon you will catch yourself doing it and not even meaning to. Your body will just start to naturally seek this activity and alert your mind that it's time to move.

Variations:

Take a class, watch a video, grab a partner and do a twirl. Put on some music and go with the flow, or don't go with it. Dance however you want to dance even if that means off-beat. Anything here counts and will mark an effort that will show. Eventually you will become more and more comfortable and surprise yourself the first time you catch yourself dancing without caring if anyone sees you. Gasp, I know it sounds fun, because it is.

How to build it into your routine:

Like we did before, start now. Get up, shake something and sit back down. If it made you smile even a little then you're getting what I'm talking about. At the very least I can almost guarantee it didn't set you off, and that's about all we are aiming for in the beginning of this am I right?!

Chapter 16

Morning Wake-Up Song

<u>What it is and my thoughts on it:</u>

This is another one that you will most likely think is silly but again, give it a try and after sometime when you can feel the results of it, it'll seem less awkward. **Routine for some people with anxiety can be crucial. There's something soothing and relieving about knowing exactly how the next thirty minutes of your day is going to pan out and can sometimes set a positive tone of reassurance for the rest of the day. This morning routine is to take the thinking factor out, so that your mind can go to more positive places.**

Think of a song that makes you happy, makes you want to move and/or has a positive message and make this your morning jam. Every morning you play this song as you wake up and are doing your thing. The positivity and the energy it can give you just might replace that cup of coffee after some time.

<u>Why I think it works:</u>

There's something about music that pretty much no one can deny. It makes your emotions just sky rocket whether they be happy or sad. Some songs have even been studied to show that when people listen to them and are told to sit still, they literally can't. Think of this notion and I wouldn't be surprised that when your specific song ends you're not quick to find another one to keep listening. Sometimes I even put my song on repeat. **If you have good lyrics and a message being blasted into**

your face in the morning it makes it a little harder to be so down in the dumps. Truthfully.

How I do it:

Find your song, or a few of them even. Take your phone and put the song on as soon as you get up, while you're laying in bed, or when you start brushing your teeth and then start your routine. My routine is the same every morning. I get up, go to the bathroom, brush my teeth, floss, and do my face regime. Then I brush my hair and then it's time to let the dog out. When we come back I feed him while I take my vitamins and medicine and then I check and water my plants. This whole process takes about twenty minutes and is the same every morning. I listen to only one song in the morning because while we are outside walking I like to enjoy nature and the sounds around me, practicing my mindfulness. This brief part of my day is honestly the most peaceful and I can't help but think it's partially because of the redundancy, or the extra pep in my step that the song inevitably puts into my day. I switch it up every now and again depending on how much of a boost I think I'll need that day. I also have a few to choose from in case I want or need more than one song to get me pumped up for the day.

Variations:

If you somehow don't like music or you need to be quiet in the mornings so you don't wake others, grab headphones or instead of music you could read a passage, a poem, look at some art or even watch a daily sermon or motivational speaker for some inspiration. Anything that is positive and can shake any thoughts you might have that are dreading the coming day. Even if the rest of your day is horrible you can say that for five minutes you were at some level of peace today and that is where it all can start. **We are looking for moments to build into minutes, to build into hours, then into days. Don't be discouraged at anything that doesn't happen instantly.** Remember, give each one of these techniques you try, a month. If you give it an honest go every day for a month then maybe it's not for you, but that doesn't mean one or all of these others won't work so keep searching.

How to build it into your routine:

A lot of us use the alarm on our phone to wake us up. If this is you, then this is easy. Set a secondary alarm for once you're up and when this one goes off this is your reminder to put on that music. You can also leave a note on your mirror in your bathroom or on your nightstand. Somewhere that you will see it in the morning and keep you reminded to complete this task before moving on. If you're doing the morning journal then use that as a reminder. As soon as you're done writing you can play the tunes. Like everything else, it can take some time to adjust and build but eventually just like brushing your teeth it will become second nature. Keep it extra spicy by rotating what song you play especially if you want to go off of the type of day you're having. For instance, what you play on the weekends can be different from what you play on a work day.

Chapter 17

Stretching

<u>What it is and my thoughts on it:</u>

Stretching is exactly what it sounds like. This doesn't have to be a mad task or timely one. A lot of us stretch when we first wake up and are still in bed but I want you to take this a notch further. As with any type of movement and exercise check with your doctor first but if you're cleared, check out a few yoga poses for beginners to stretch your back, neck and shoulders. You can even find ones that can be done in your bed as a way to get your blood flowing and as a way to wake up some before you even get up. Combine the last chapter and this one, and while you're laying in bed, crank that morning jam and do some stretching for five minutes or until the song is over. You haven't even gotten out of bed yet and you've already knocked out two techniques. This is a perfect example of how to arrange these in a way where you literally need five minutes to start. That's it and this is an example of how you can double up and do two at once. **When you start to feel the benefits, trust me when I say you will begin to find the time to prioritize your day to fit in more of these activities as well as begin to get creative in how to do more than one a day.**

<u>Why I think it works:</u>

Any type of movement gets your heart going and your blood flowing a little more to your brain and organs. It's simply a way to wake up your body and to say, "Hey, let's get going we have a full day ahead." Some people drink coffee or eat a hearty breakfast, so why not include a little physical activity as well into your routine for one more added piece to get you going. Some of us need all the help we can get in the morning and I highly recommend adapting the mindset of, "Don't knock it until you try it."

Movement and exercise have an overwhelming foundation of evidence that they do good things for your body. It's something we're taught in school when we're little and quite frankly the reminders never stop. Everyone promotes activity on some level as long as it's doctor approved, so get going. We're not talking anything extensive or even difficult. If anything stretching can warm up those muscles and actually feel really good. Stretching can also reduce your chances of injury by increasing your flexibility and even a little bit of strength depending on what type of stretching you're doing. Balance and core strength can also benefit as well. A strong core can reduce back pain, especially lower back pain so amidst all these reasons clearly you can find one that suits you. This can be a great segue into yoga. Start with just stretching in the morning and then find a few poses to incorporate. Focus on poses that are done laying down so you don't even have to get out of bed.

How I do it:

My favorite stretch is a yoga pose called child's pose. It gets my upper back, shoulders, and neck all stretched out so I can loosen those tightened joints that have gotten stiff overnight. I like to stretch some of my leg muscles and I also make sure I do some neck exercises to again loosen some tension and tight muscles that result from sleeping for eight hours. Yeah, I said eight hours. That's how this woman sleeps now-a-days, like a rock for eight hours. It is a real thing people.

Variations:

Not too many variations, just a matter of what you do and how long. Again, this can be viewed as a mini yoga session so it can be the perfect introduction to starting that habit or at least testing it out.

How to build it into your routine:

Start while you're in bed. Again, naturally we stretch our arms out or something while still laying in bed. When you do this take it as your reminder and just do one more stretch before getting out of bed. This can take 30 seconds. If you don't have 30 seconds or a few minutes to spare each morning, then you are the prime candidate here that seriously needs to alter their morning routine, as it sounds super rushed and then you wonder why you have anxiety, just saying.

Chapter 18

Exercise

<u>What it is and my thoughts on it:</u>

Speaking of stretching, exercise is taking it up one more notch. Make sure you have clearance from your doctor to do exercise and find out exactly what kind you are permitted to do to prevent injury. If at any time you are exercising and you feel light headed, your heart is racing or palpitating, or you feel really hot and it's hard to breathe then stop immediately and sit down. If symptoms persist contact a medical professional. Don't take this lightly, I've had my whole face go pale and my heart rate increase to 185 after just doing five minutes on the treadmill and not even at a fast pace. When you have anxiety sometimes your heart rate can naturally be abnormally high so physical activity that your body is not used to can make this worse. Find what works for you and experiment further with that. Some people need cardio while others need a more calm approach with slower but concentrated movements like we talked about in previous chapters.

<u>Why I think it works:</u>

Exercise has been known to release endorphins which make us feel good, productive, and accomplished. I don't know of anyone who has ever worked out, and afterwards regretted it, so just give it a shot. It can be a very daunting and difficult thing to get into the habit of doing but it can become a very addicting habit especially once you start seeing and feeling results. When you look good, you feel good, and your inner peace with yourself goes up and trust me, inner bliss shows on the outside as well.

How I do it:

Due to some injuries a while ago, I have experimented for years on different exercises and what my body can tolerate. I can walk but running is too high impact for me. I'm not a fan of swimming but I would like to be one day because it's known to be easy on the joints and body. For now, I pretty much stick to my physical therapy exercises which for the average person probably wouldn't seem like exercise at all, but for my body it most definitely is. **This is a perfect example of how we need to stop paying so much attention to what others are doing. Who cares what you're doing or how tough it is perceived? Do what you can within your limits.** I use a lot of stretch bands and also movements that use my own body weight as resistance. Eventually, I will get to where I used to be as far as being able to do boot camps and intense circuit training, which was always my favorite, but for now I have to listen to my body no matter how frustrating that might be. I've managed to lose over fifty-five pounds, and none of it was due to heavy exercise. So besides being toned and having definition, I'm not missing out on much anyway. I don't want to dismiss how credible this technique is, I'm trying to stress to only do what your body can tolerate and trust that it still counts as exercise.

Variations:

Physical therapy, water aerobics, workouts while laying down for stability and form as well as gentle yoga and beginner levels of programs are all low key ways to introduce your body into this new adventure. You have to start somewhere and by doing that you are already ahead of the game so pat yourself on the back.

How to build it into your routine:

Set aside five minutes at any point in your day. In the morning before anything else, in the evening before you wind down to work out the stress of the day, right before you shower so you can clean off that sweat you might produce, or even while you're watching TV. I used to watch TV and every commercial break stop to do a pushup or sit-up. You can laugh all you want but even doing just one pushup is one more than most people did that day. The trick behind this is, half of the time once you're in the position you'll end up doing more than one. I told you I get sneaky with my techniques.

Chapter 19

Vision Boards

<u>What it is and my thoughts on it:</u>

I love these. This is such a fun project to do with a close friend or a group of people while having a get together with some beverages and light snacks. Poster boards are super cheap and so is glue and every one has a pair of scissors. Find that stash of magazines you've been meaning to read and get to clipping. Find things that make you smile and happy and things that you want in your life. As usual — say it with me — "Nothing is too small or insignificant." Whatever you want in your life, find a picture or a word that represents it, and put it on your board. Once you're done, put this board somewhere you can see it almost everyday and focus on it. **This helps you see why you're living, why you're working so hard and why it's important to stay positive and focused on these techniques you're incorporating. This will help you manifest things and to also highlight things you're grateful for each day.**

<u>Why I think it works:</u>

Talk about positivity, this exercise can get those dream wheels turning and help unlock what it is you really want in life. It can help you uncover desires you never even knew you had and get those juices going about what it is you might need to start doing to get closer to these goals that you have. These pictures and words, which can give you empowerment, can help you when you're having a rough day to remember how insignificant some of our worries are as well as how important it is to keep moving forward.

How I do it:

I went out and bought the materials and scheduled a day with a friend to commit to this project. Making a vision board can take some time so this was to get the foundation working and then we'd finish them at home. There are no rules just flip through a magazine and cut out whatever hits you and resonates with what makes you happy. There is no such thing as a bad vision board as long as it's not dangerous or violent of course. This is about positivity, goals, dreams, and aspirations beyond what you even think is possible.

Variations:

If you feel this is a more private thing to do then just do it at home while watching tv or listening to some music. You can even start with a mini one or just start looking through magazines and writing down things that you want out of life. This can be similar to a bucket list or a life plan. A vision board is simply more visual therefore it resonates on a different level, and can then instill in your mind that it is possible. You can even start with only a few pictures and continue to keep adding as your life develops and what you want becomes more clear.

How to build it into your routine:

This isn't a daily thing as much as maybe an activity to do every few months or even once a year. If you have trouble finding pictures and can't fill a full board, go with the small option and add to it occasionally. **Your dreams and goals will absolutely change as you grow as a person and in the best way possible. The more confident you become and the less anxiety you have, then your ability to dream bigger will**

start to emerge. This doesn't have to take place of your original dreams, just simply add to them. Once you accomplish some of these you will feel such a sense of achievement and success that it will only increase the drive you have to succeed and break down any walls that are in your path to greatness.

Chapter 20

Therapists (all of them)

<u>What it is and my thoughts on it:</u>

Therapists are a thing that some might be embarrassed about and that is absolutely understandable. There is such a stigma and association with mental illnesses that most people hide the fact that they see a therapist. The reality is that psychologists and psychiatrists are everywhere, and there are tens of thousands of them across the country so clearly someone is using their services. It's just usually something people don't talk about for fear of judgement. In reality, these professionals know what they're doing and they can help you make drastic changes if you find the right therapist to work with you. Just like everything else we have discussed, everyone is different so the therapist that you need could be different from the one that I need. **Don't be afraid to keep switching professionals until you find one that you click with and can be honest with which is a huge, important factor for making progress and having breakthroughs. It's your money! Keep searching until you find one who listens to you and that you feel is truly helping you make progress.**

<u>Why I think it works:</u>

There is definitely some science behind why this works and how having someone support you, who isn't judging you, can be such a nice feeling. At first you might think some of their tactics seem odd, or the homework they give you might seem trivial or senseless, but just give them a chance. These therapists are not there to waste your time and they are not just making up things for you to try. The methods they've learned to help people have been studied and really do work. So, even if it seems annoying, give it a shot. They are experts for a reason so find a way to trust them. If you can't trust them, then you need to find a new therapist.

How I do it:

At one point I had three therapists and I had zero shame in it. I had an in-person therapist I saw once a week, a virtual therapist I talked to over the phone once a week, and a third one that I checked in with every two to three months. For me, this was necessary and although I absolutely dreaded these appointments sometimes, I never left them feeling bad. In fact, I always felt better and relieved upon leaving. After some time, I even started to enjoy them as if I was going to visit a friend. I could be honest and open and felt comfortable to the point where no topic went off limits. **This can be a pricey tool, but check with your health insurance plans as some states have mental health programs where they work with people to lower the price, some have payment plans, and there are even ones who offer free services via a health insurance program. You could have access to this amazing tool for free and not even know it, so it's worth a call to your insurance company to check your options.** I was lucky to have an insurance plan that covered this cost and considering it was free, I had absolutely no excuse to not go, and it truly changed my life. Try to find a program that works for you, and if you can, commit to more than just one month of this particular technique.

Variations:

This is where digital, virtual, or in person options can vary. Try to find someone you can trust and feel safe with. Find someone willing to work with you and at your pace. If you're religious, try going to church more often, or find a shaman, guru, or some person who you feel can offer positive advice while listening to you with zero judgement. Find a group near you of other people with anxiety who meet to discuss things with each other almost like AA. If you don't like sitting and exposing your life to strangers face-to-face, search for groups online in social media groups. You can try a health coach, life coach, and other professions which are in such abundance right now that if you look you will most definitely find someone that vibes with you that is in your price range.

How to build it into your routine:

Do a little research to find what's available in your area. Call your health insurance to find out what is included in your plan and see if there's discounted programs or even free ones for mental health. Watch inspirational videos, therapeutic speeches or something of the like online. Again, find a church or volunteer place. There's so many forms of therapy than just laying on a couch and talking about what happened when you were five years old. Personally, I like the couch method, and it worked for me, but it's all about what works for you when making this decision.

Chapter 21

Post-It Notes

<u>What it is and my thoughts on it:</u>

Post-it notes or just notes in general are another one of my favorites. It can be uncomfortable doing this depending on who you live with but imagine little notes everywhere with positive affirmations. Reminders of fun things to do or even a note that just says, "Smile." I love these but I still get embarrassed about them and take them all down when I'm expecting company. After all, they are for me and me only, and in order to put on them exactly what needs to be said, I still need privacy with them. I personally need to be completely blunt and open with what I write on these notes strung about my home, and I need to do so without any fear of being judged, so I don't leave them out for others to see.

These are the perfect way to remind yourself of all of the other things and techniques you need to be doing. There is no limit to how many you can put up or where to put them. The bathroom mirror tends to be a common one so you can read them each morning and start the day off right, as well as ending it right once you're doing your nighttime routine.

<u>Why I think it works:</u>

With having anxiety our brains are so full of fears, over-thinking, and irrational thoughts, that it can be tough to remember these positive things. We can even have a fantastic day that somehow can be erased instantly by day's end because the anxiety comes back out from the shadows in an attempt to pull us down. **These post-it notes keep everything fresh and on the surface which results in putting that anxiety fire right back out.** Affirmations are a fantastic tool that can be sometimes mocked or underrated. What I've learned is that I don't care what others think. If it keeps me out of the ER and from doing self-destructive things then I'm doing it, period.

How I do it:

I just started with one and then once I got comfortable with it, I went crazy and they were everywhere. In my kitchen, in the bathroom on the mirrors, on the walls next to my TV, on the door as I leave, and on the bathroom doors. I had everything from, "Be Happy" to "Do a Body Scan," and even ones that said, "Who gives a shit what anyone else thinks, this is about you!" Seriously, whatever works for you, and don't be afraid to be bold and honest. If you find after a while the message gets old, take it down and write a new one in its place.

Variations:

Not too many comparable techniques unless you carry around a journal with you that you can reference from time to time. If you live with someone who would either mock you or expose your innocent technique then perhaps keep them in your room only. You could keep them in a drawer and reference them when you need to. You could keep a small pad of paper in your purse to read in times of need at work or before you go into a store or other public place. You could even just hang a blank post-it and you would know what it signified, and that could also hold power, in that only you know what it means. **For me these go a long way. It's like having a friend around all the time constantly telling you nice things and complimenting**

you all the time. Get creative if you are living with someone who wouldn't understand your needs. Better yet, hand them this book when you're done with it and give them some insight into what you are dealing with. Maybe it'll help them understand you more or help them to be more compassionate if you feel you're not being heard.

How to build it into your routine:

Grab some pretty or cheery colored post-its and you guessed it, just start. Start with simple ones like, "Have a great day" or "You will be ok." No comment or affirmation is insignificant, too small, or ineffective. This is about you. What works for someone else might make your anxiety worse and vice versa so write what feels good for you.

Chapter 22

Where I Am Now

Since I began this journey of really finding a routine for myself and experimenting with these methods it has been a rollercoaster of emotions to say the least. Some days I feel fantastic and know it's all working and feel just so at peace I can hardly believe it. Other days, I still feel defeated or no matter how hard I try, that enemy is just too strong for me that day. Don't let this discourage you from starting. **Understanding that there is the chance that days like this might always exist is extremely important for our minds to do. Remember step one, acceptance.** You'll slowly begin to feel the good days outweighing the bad and this can be a huge progression marker. On that good day I celebrate it a little more and then also remind myself that, "If tomorrow happens to be a bad day, I still need to stay on track." This sets almost a subconscious tone in my mind, and I like to think it gives the enemy a heads up that I'm already prepped for it, and I'm not going down without a fight should it try to ruin my day. I can have great weeks in a row and then almost have a full day where I forget that I might still be vulnerable, and in that moment I swear the devil begins to wake up. When I notice trends like extra lack of motivation, abnormal fatigue, or inability to focus, these are key signs that an attack can be as far away as a week or as close as the next day. **In these moments of awareness is when we need to hit the routine extra hard and stay aggressive and even go beyond a normal day's routine to reverse what's being tested on us.**

If we begin to feel "off," it's usually because something is. So when this happens, we have to be our own little detectors and run through each part of us and our day to find out what's dragging us down. Think of what you ate that day. Food is a huge factor and is never addressed as much as it needs to be. Maybe something you ate that week threw you off, like having to much sugar or caffeine. Did you stay up late? Sleep is also underrated and extremely important in having a healthy mind. How's your physical activity been? Did you miss a few days last week that are catching up to you and now you're feeling sluggish? Keep going just like this until it clicks, did you not do enough self-care? Did you need more meditation? Did you not practice mindfulness as much as you normally do? And so on, and eventually you will find an answer. As you learn more about your body and mind and how they work, these answers will come more easily. **If you've had anxiety your entire life, it's not going to go away overnight. Greatness takes time and focus. If you just commit to it, I can promise you, it most definitely is worth it!**

Since my findings and practicing of these techniques, I have genuinely become a different person. One that I was afraid to become, but that I am glad I persisted forward with in my efforts. Since becoming this new version of myself, I've gotten four tattoos, I've moved 1500+ miles halfway across the country to my dream city of Austin, I went back to school, graduated, and am still continuing my education with classes online. I've reconnected with friends and family whom I lost contact with for years because they had a hard time processing my condition or understanding my stubborn and unwise way of healing. I've made some incredible new friends who are able to offer support unlike anything I've ever experienced simply because I wasn't afraid to seek what I deserved. Hell, I even wrote a book and have started my own company. The list goes on and on and my gratitude journal pages are always full! I feel more free and happier than I've ever been or even thought possible. I have less attacks and a more positive way of viewing the world. I've even noticed my dreams are different now that I am more comfortable with myself. I don't have these embarrassing nightmares anymore where people are constantly making fun of me. Instead my dreams are happy and just more calm, if that even makes sense. I wake up ready to go and I don't feel groggy or run down anymore, I feel rested and happy. All my life, all I knew was this life of anxiety. For over 30 years I put up with it and was too intimidated to try to fight. Once I found just one thing that helped, I began to gain confidence and self-worth, thinking that I could get better at handling this just by taking better care of myself and taking the time to do what I needed to do to break free. I still have a prison in my mind, I just choose to stay outside of it. I choose to keep my thoughts under control and to focus on the blue skies ahead — even if those blue skies are only seen while looking through the barbed-wire fence.

Chapter 23

Keeping Up With The Routine, What Happens If You Stop?

Trust that this whole adventure you're about to embark on is important enough to keep in your life forever, at least on some level. I know people who have gone years without attacks and then suddenly have one and can't explain why it occurred. The fact that this is a common thing to happen, is enough to validate me into just accepting that this new life is something that is my own now. To go backwards is so easy, but it's not worth it, and it's nowhere near as fun. The tougher route is harder but it is beyond worth the results, and I have to remind myself of that sometimes daily still.

I had been good for quite sometime and then I moved and all my tools and things were packed away and I was without them for over a month. I thought I'd be strong enough to maintain and hold onto this new self, yet I was unfortunately and quickly, proved wrong. I almost was in disbelief as to how far back I receded and how fast it happened. I thought I would have enough distractions with a new environment, lots of unpacking, and loads of stuff to do and explore, that it wouldn't matter but boy was I wrong. It was almost instant. Within a couple weeks it was as if I had barely started and within a month, it was as if everything got completely erased and I was back to square one.

Imagine if you were super diligent with an exercise routine as well as with your diet, for months. You had reached a visible transformation in your physical strength, tone, endurance, and feeling of overall wellness. Then for a month you decided to sit on the couch and eat nothing but junk and fast food. Can you imagine how awful you'd begin to feel and how quickly that feeling would set in? Well, it's the same thing here, it just applies to our minds. I have learned I need to be aware of this and recognize this so I can be sure to never get too far away from the goal at hand. There isn't really a finish line here. You can feel amazing, but maintaining that feeling is always going to require focus. It will also slowly begin to not feel like work, which is awesome. Some of these are extremely enjoyable to be honest and a decent amount are very minimal in how much time they take so they don't have an overwhelming feel to them in my day. I did have to have somewhat of a strict schedule right in the beginning; however, I felt better within days which then immediately makes it feel less like a task or a necessity, and transfers over to a feeling of anticipation and even excitement to do these each day.

The nice thing about these techniques is that there are so many that on any given day if you don't feel like doing one, you just pick another. The options are endless so this too helps make it seem less of a chore and more of a fun activity. You can go a day where you do the minimal amount of tasks, but make sure the next day you double up just to be sure progress isn't lost. It might take some adjusting and trial and error to see which ones work for you but trust me, it's worth it. Give yourself this chance at a happier life and you too will find yourself never looking back.

Conclusion

To create something life-changing can be difficult. It requires diligence and strong efforts, but rarely does that not result in something remarkable. You deserve this. Who cares if you require a little more work than someone else does in order to be happy? Why would you not want to take care of yourself to feel better? We all deserve to be happy. We all deserve this life.

Every human being has tragedy of some shape and size in their life. Maybe ours is more persistent in that it shows up daily as opposed to less frequent, but trust that there is some form of tragedy inside everyone. Their's might be less intense or more dormant, but it is there. There is no longer a reason for us to think that we are alone in this illness. There are over 40 million people who suffer from a mental illness. We are anything but alone. If ever in a given moment, after you've accepted your anxiety, began a routine of techniques for yourself, and are feeling better, you still feel alone, please have the ability to acknowledge that this is ok to feel, but that it most certainly isn't the truth. If you have a hard time reversing this thought, that's ok, just then know that even if you are "alone", that you alone are all you will ever need to make it through this. You alone are enough. You alone are enough to survive this and to fight. In fact for some, until you see you can survive it alone, it might remain difficult to survive among the crowds. So I stress for you to try these tools for yourself. Build your sense of comfort within yourself and do this for you and your future self. **Use outside resources but know that the internal ones are the ones that heal the deepest of wounds for that is where the pain hides. You are deserving, you are enough and you are worthy of a better life.** If you or anyone else ever makes you question this, then power through that moment, be the bigger person, and tell them that they too are enough, and then go on to remind yourself once more that, "You alone are enough."

About The Author

Erica Rose Goldsmith is originally from Baltimore, MD, but now resides in Austin, TX. She went to UMBC as well as HCC in Baltimore and Columbia, MD, respectively. She studied Biochemistry and Molecular Biology receiving an Associates degree in Life Sciences and an Associates degree in Laboratory Sciences - Biotechnology. More recently, she graduated from the Institute of Integrative Nutrition receiving the title Integrative Nutrition Health Coach. She since then has become an Internationally Certified Health Coach as well as a Board Certified Holistic Health Practitioner. She's the owner of Revive and Renew You, LLC, where she focuses on her client's needs to help them on their journey of transformation. Few topics are off limits; however, she specializes in weight loss, anxiety, trauma and spirituality.

She has two brothers, a dog, and loves to cook and bake. She also enjoys writing, puzzles of any sort, a good movie, and of course music. Her passion for helping others comes from her own extreme life experiences and knowing that if she had the knowledge she does now about this and other illnesses, that perhaps she could've saved herself and others a lot of sadness and pain amidst many other emotions. This is her goal on this path she now pursues — To help as many people as she can to learn ways to combat this disease before they lose control and all hope the way she did. Hopefully, you have found some help and guidance in reading this book. At the very least, hopefully you feel less alone.

www.ingramcontent.com/pod-product-compliance
Lightning Source LLC
Chambersburg PA
CBHW070813100426
42742CB00012B/2350